ROUTLEDGE LIBRARY EDITIONS: DISCOURSE ANALYSIS

Volume 6

COMMON DISCOURSE PARTICLES IN ENGLISH CONVERSATION

COMMON DISCOURSE PARTICLES IN ENGLISH CONVERSATION

LAWRENCE C. SCHOURUP

LONDON AND NEW YORK

First published in 1985 by Garland Publishing, Inc

This edition first published in 2017
by Routledge
2 Park Square, Milton Park, Abingdon, Oxon OX14 4RN

and by Routledge
711 Third Avenue, New York, NY 10017

Routledge is an imprint of the Taylor & Francis Group, an informa business

© 1985 Lawrence C. Schourup

All rights reserved. No part of this book may be reprinted or reproduced or utilised in any form or by any electronic, mechanical, or other means, now known or hereafter invented, including photocopying and recording, or in any information storage or retrieval system, without permission in writing from the publishers.

Trademark notice: Product or corporate names may be trademarks or registered trademarks, and are used only for identification and explanation without intent to infringe.

British Library Cataloguing in Publication Data
A catalogue record for this book is available from the British Library

ISBN: 978-1-138-22094-2 (Set)
ISBN: 978-1-315-40146-1 (Set) (ebk)
ISBN: 978-1-138-22479-7 (Volume 6) (hbk)
ISBN: 978-1-138-22480-3 (Volume 6) (pbk)
ISBN: 978-1-315-40158-4 (Volume 6) (ebk)

Publisher's Note
The publisher has gone to great lengths to ensure the quality of this reprint but points out that some imperfections in the original copies may be apparent.

Disclaimer
The publisher has made every effort to trace copyright holders and would welcome correspondence from those they have been unable to trace.

Common Discourse Particles in English Conversation

Lawrence C. Schourup

Garland Publishing, Inc. ■ New York & London
1985

Library of Congress Cataloging in Publication Data

Schourup, Lawrence C. (Lawrence Clifford), 1947–
  Common discourse particles in English conversation.

  (Outstanding dissertations in linguistics)
  Revision of thesis (Ph.D.)—Ohio State University, 1982.
  Bibliography: p.
  1. English language—Spoken English. 2. English
language—Particles. I. Title. II. Series.
PE1321.S35 1985   421'.5   85-10374
ISBN 0-8240-5439-3 (alk. paper)

© 1985 by Lawrence C. Schourup
All rights reserved

The volumes in this series are printed on
acid-free, 250-year-life paper.

Printed in the United States of America

CONTENTS

Preface   v

List of Symbols   ix

1   Introduction

    1.1   General Remarks   1
    1.2   Covert Thinking in Conversation   4
    1.3   Three 'Worlds' of the Speaker   7
    1.4   Routinization   10
    1.5   Use of Speech Materials   13
    1.6   Outline of Remaining Chapters   15

2   Evincives

    2.1   Interjections and Evincives   17
    2.2   Evincives in Quotations   22
    2.2.1   Well and Oh in Quotations   22
    2.3   Enquoting   30
    2.4   Quotation   31
    2.5   Summary   35

3   'Like'

    3.1   Like in Conversation   37
    3.2   Like Introducing Direct Discourse   43
    3.3   Like After Questions   47
    3.4   The 'For Example' Use   48
    3.5   Like as an Interjection   52
    3.6   It's Like   59
    3.7   Conclusion   61

4   'Well'

    4.1   Introduction   64
    4.2   Well Before Exclamations   67
    4.3   Well Introducing Direct Discourse   69
    4.4   Topic Shifting   71
    4.5   Well Before Answers   73
    4.6   Well Before Questions   76
    4.7   Well and Self-Repair   77
    4.8   Well and Other-Repair   81
    4.9   Sentence-Final Well   84

- iii -

4.10	Reduced _Well_	85
4.11	_Well_ and Narrative Elision	86
4.12	_Well_ and 'Intension'	88
4.13	Conclusion	90

5 'You Know'

5.1	Preliminary Remarks	94
5.2	YK as a Truth Parenthetical	96
5.3	YK and Properties of Truth Parentheticals	97
5.4	Evidence for two Types of YK	99
5.5	The Use of YKb	102
5.6	A Third YK?	106
5.7	Discourse Functions of YKb	107
5.7.1	Topic Introduction	107
5.7.2	Topic Tracking	110
5.7.3	YKb and Repair	120
5.8	YKb as a 'Sociocentric Sequence'	125
5.9	Interrogative YK	128
5.10	YK and Turn Taking	130
5.11	Distribution of YK: Some Quantitative Results	135
5.12	Conclusion	138

6 The Role of Discourse Particles in Conversation

6.1	General Remarks	141
6.2	_Now_	145
6.3	_I mean_	147
6.4	_Mind You_	148
6.5	_Sort o(f)_, _Kind o(f)_, _An(d) Stuff_, _An(d) Everything_, _An(d) so on_, etc.	149
6.6	Interjections	150
6.7	Types of Disclosure Functions	152
6.8	General Summary	154

Footnotes	157
References	168

PREFACE

While, in the narrowest sense, the subject matter
of this dissertation is English discourse particle function, it is also concerned with the model of communicative
events that such an investigation seems to require, in
which conversants' private thoughts are as much a part
of the conversational proocedings as are their words and
other actions. To refer to communicative events in this
way invites the objection that one is dealing with the
unknowable. This objection is, however, a methodological one; it arises in the attempt to gain 'concessions'
from nature by exposing patterns in observable data.

There is another view of language, somewhat closer
to the experience of speaking, in which it is taken as
unremarkably true that speakers are thinking to themselves
as they speak, and in which the resulting selectivity
of observable data is taken in stride. In this other,
speaker-based view, what is displayed or inferable from
display does not constitute all of what is happening when
people interact. If, as I have claimed in this study,
the discourse particles that pervade spontaneous speech
relate observable to unobservable aspects of the conversational process[*], then by frequent use of such particles
speakers convey ongoing concern for what they themselves
and their interlocutors are <u>not</u> indicating on the discourse
surface, and in so doing show that they regard themselves
and others not as mindless beacons emitting signals, but
as complex organisms whose behavior goes beyond impulse.

---

[*]The terms 'observable/unobservable', as they are generaly
used, assume a 'third party' reference point; the terms
'displayed/undisplayed' are neutral in this respect.

- v -

To enlarge on this view, one might look elsewhere
in conversation for indications of what is unsaid. One
might, for example, explore the parallel between the kinds
of phenomena discussed in this dissertation and a use
of intonation mentioned by Schegloff and Sacks (1973).
They consider the case of a person waiting to take an
elevator down, who , when an elevator finally arrives,
sees that it is going up, hesitates, and then says, "I
guess I _will_ wait." The contrastive stress on _will_ displays the speaker's "prior, now abandoned, decision to
'go along for the ride'" (321).

Or one might pursue the idea that speakers sometimes
engage in a "group think process" (Stubbs 1983:193) in
which they actively try to work out what they have in
mind.

Research along these avenues, and others suggested
in Chapters 1 and 6 of this dissertation, can clarify
the way in which speakers relate to thought when they
speak. Such research must work, as in the present study,
with observable data. But to approach these matters with
a view too narrowly constrained by one's methodological
preoccupation with 'third party' observation, would be
to ingnore the central fact that speakers see themselves
as engaged in an activity involving unknowns--that they
orient to each other with equal concern for outward behavior and for what they and others, to whatever extent
and for whatever reasons, leave unexpressed. The implication that the analysis of conversation will always
be inadequate to the task of explicating particular discourse surfaces might be found either irritating or in-
triguing. That such analyses do not often provide complete
or compelling answers to the question (asked in regard
to an utterance), "Why this here?", I take as an indication
of just how much iceberg is still down there.

The text of this dissertation appears here in revised form. The original manuscript, published with few corrections as Ohio State University Working Papers in Linguistics #28 (1983), contains a number of unclear passages, inconsistencies, misnumberings, and other distractions. The present revision is an attempt to clarify the original; no attempt has been made to incorporate the results of more recent work on discourse particles, which seemed beyond the intentions of the Garland series.

It has seemed to me for some time that the term 'evincive', coined in the text, is best or most prototypically applied to items such as well (Ch. 4) and Oh (Chs. 2 and 6), and only with diminished explanatory value to like (Ch. 3). In revising, I have nevertheless retained the original designation of like as an evincive, since it seems to me at least related to the prototypical cases, even if it is admittedly somewhat odd to refer to what is unexpressed in the case of like as 'thinking', and even if like shows less syntactic independence than well and oh. Similarly, the case for there being a single core use for each particle is, I feel, far stronger for well and you know than for like, though, here again, the original line of argument has been retained.

In bringing this work to completion, I benefited greatly from discussions with Arnold Zwicky, whose scholarly example has been a continuing encouragement over many years. His comments several times caused me to think more deeply about the matters discussed here and, more than once, to broaden my perspective.

I would also like to thank Robert Fox, Michael Geis, and Brian Joseph for reading a draft of this dissertation and offering valuable suggestions, and those who discussed specific topics with me: William Boslego, Douglas Fuller, Richard Garner, Carol Jean Godby, John

Nerbonne, Joseph Pettigrew, Deborah Schaffer, and Rachel
Schaffer.

I am indebted to these people for sharing their
thoughts with me, whatever the use (or misuse) of their
ideas in the final form of this dissertation.

I would also like to acknowledge here a luncheon
remark by Francisco Varela of Naropa Institute, in which
he first pointed out to me the great inherent fascination
of conversation studies.

Several others contributed to this work through their
patience and friendship. Special thanks are due in this
regard to my father, William H. Schourup; and to Deborah
Andersen, Chester Drake, Carolyn Kurtz, Jacquelyn McKee,
Stephen D. Miller, Marlene Payha, Karen Shockey, Helen
Thiry, Jeffrey Thomas, and Richard Weiner.

This dissertation is dedicated to the memory of my
mother, Yvonne Mierlot Schourup (1924-1973).

LIST OF SYMBOLS[*]

...   indicates part of an utterance elided; can indicate pause

.   indicates falling ('declarative') intonation

,   indicates level ('continuing') intonation

?   indicates rising ('interrogative') intonation

( )   when empty, indicates material unintelligible to transcriber; enclosing a complete word or words, indicates transcriber uncertainty (as can //); containing part of a word, indicates sounds corresponding to enclosed letters were not pronounced; enclosing h internal in an otherwise complete word, indicates a 'laugh token' (brief voiceless exhalation); enclosing numbers, indicates length in seconds of an unfilled pause

( ) (( ))   enclose transcriber comments. ( ) may also enclose phonetic transcriptions and duration in seconds of an unfilled pause

:   indicates an overlong segment or syllable

underscoring   indicates heavy stress

! CAPS   indicate extremely heavy stress

=   within a single turn, indicates preceding item was spoken as if closely linked with following item; used at the end of a speaking turn and repeated at beginning of same speaker's next turn (or continuation), indicates that what precedes the first = is linked to what follows the second =

-       with space to right, indicates preceding item was broken off or spoken haltingly; with spaces both to left and right, indicates an unmeasured pause

[/   indicate point at which talk by one speaker began to overlap that of another speaker

]   indicates the end of the overlap

[*]See Chapter 1 §5.

- ix -

CHAPTER ONE

INTRODUCTION

1.1 General Remarks

This is a study of several common items in English
conversation known variously as 'discourse particles',
'interjections', 'discourse markers', and less respect-
fully as 'hesitations' or 'fillers'. Attention will
be directed primarily to analyses of like, well and you
know, but the larger concern of this study is the entire
set of items of which these are members, and some attention will therefore also be given to related items, including I mean, now, oh, hey and aha. The term discourse
particles will be used throughout the study to refer
to the words and expressions under discussion. The term
is intended as a neutral label for these items that
avoids a priori judgments on their function or grammatical classification but does indicate that they are primarily discourse phenomena. The general program of the
study is to examine the discourse functions of particles
at length and then propose a framework in which their
uses individually make sense and in which revealing com-
parisons can be made between them. A correct understanding of discourse particles, it will be claimed, requires
a widening of the usual purview of conversation studies.

The need for work on discourse particles is apparent
on examining almost any transcript of spontaneous English
conversation. The repertoire of favored forms may differ
from speaker to speaker, but in general instances of
like, well, you know and similar items abound in conversation. Despite their great frequency of occurrence, however, until recently only crude attempts had been made
to characterize the role of these items in conversation.

- 1 -

By many researchers they were dismissed as meaningless and presumed to lack interesting distributional features; others offered tentative analyses applicable only to a narrow range of the items' occurrence; and in the popular view such items have tended to be stigmatized as verbal 'crutches' used by those deficient in speaking ability. Reviews of these early treatments are found in James (1974) and Goldberg (1980).

The former neglect of these items seems to have been due largely to the fact that their appearance is for the most part limited to conversation, a use of language itself neglected until recent years (despite the widespread availability of tape recorders since the 1950's). But the difficulties discourse particles can present when examined by introspection have no doubt also been an obstacle to research. Questions to informants concerning the use or meaning of well, for example, are apt to elicit only puzzlement or a list of examples. It will be suggested below that there may be a deeper reason for these introspective difficulties than the commonly noted tendency for such items to be spoken more or less unconsciously.

During the last decade, which has seen a sudden flourishing of interest in studies of conversation, the sheer frequency of these items in talk and the lack of an adequate account of their function have led to several exploratory investigations. All of this recent work begins from the now no longer disputed observation that such items differ from each other in distribution and use and so cannot be simply regarded as 'fillers'. The studies now available fall into two broad categories, according to the type of data used. Studies of the first type are based almost entirely on intuitive evidential statements (e.g., James 1972, 1973, 1974, 1978; Lakoff

1973; Hines 1977; Murray 1979). The most ambitious work of this kind is James (1972) which specifies semantic and distributional properties of such items as oh, ah and say (designating them as 'interjections'--the traditional categorization for forms that resist inclusion in the 'sentential' word classes). Another group of studies attempts to isolate the conventional functions of discourse particles by examining their use in tapes and transcripts of natural conversation. Important studies of this kind have been carried out by Crystal and Davy (1975), Goldberg (1980), Svartvik (1980), and Schiffrin (1981b). Each of the studies mentioned above will be discussed, as relevant, in later chapters.

The present study will use both recorded conversations and introspective data in attempting to identify a core use for each of several discourse particles. It will be shown that when the basic use of each item has been correctly isolated, an understanding of the variety of discourse functions that item is capable of serving proceeds directly from considering how its core use is interpretable in particular conversational contexts. In addition the general function of discourse particles will be characterized by showing how they constitute the range of conventionalized responses in English to what will be called the problem of disclosure. Briefly, the disclosure problem is that unexpressed thinking engaged in by conversants concurrent with their participation in a conversation may be communicatively relevant to their displayed verbal and other actions. It will be claimed that each discourse particle considered mediates in a specific way between the current undisclosed thinking of conversants and what they are currently doing in the way of talk and other behavior.

Although the position to be developed in the present

work refers to 'undisclosed thinking', the claims made will not depend on inquisitions into what any particular speaker was thinking on a specific occasion. To do so would rob this inquiry of its empirical foundation. Matters undisclosed will be left, as they must, to the imagination. On the other hand, one would not do well to deny the existence of unexpressed thinking, and for this reason it will be of use here to briefly survey the nature and importance of the 'invisible' aspects of conversation.

1.2 Covert Thinking in Conversation

It is intuitively obvious that conversants do not say aloud everything that crosses their minds. Rather, they select some 'mental contents' as appropriate to verbalize and retain others. Or unexpressed thinking may be temporarily 'shelved' and introduced later when-- perhaps through attempts at redirecting the conversa- tion--its verbalization in some form has become appro- priate. It is unimportant to the real matter of this distinction between talk and covert thinking whether what is deferred or left unexpressed is 'silent speech' or instead some kind of nonlinguistic or quasilinguistic mental activity; in either case what gets spoken is only part of what comes to mind.

Numerous aspects of conversational behavior are nonspontaneous and therefore point to a divergence of talk and thought. The many recent explorations of conver- sational structure by sociologists (Goffman, Sacks, Scheg- loff, Jefferson, and others) have been helpful in estab- lishing that speakers do not practice an absolute extem- poraneity--voicing their thoughts as they arise--but judiciously retain, shape, and sequentially place them in ways that often display considerable gamesmanship.

There is room within the tonus[1] of a conversation for much private thought. We form overall judgments, plan provisional responses, rank and revise them, store questions, foresee the need for further conversations, and so on, and routinely do these things while someone else is talking, or while we ourselves hold the turn.

Speakers sometimes _report_ thoughts as having occurred covertly during talk by introducing their subsequent verbalization of them with a prefix like those in (1):[2]

> (1) I thought of this while you were/I was talking...
> I was going to say...
> Your mentioning cholera a moment ago reminded me...

It is not unacceptable, and is often expected, that conversants ponder what is said, and they may affect this by head scratching or chin pulling, as well as by the considered responsiveness of what they say. Private thought is troublesome only if it becomes preoccupation.

Items like _What in the world!_ represent another way speakers naturalize covert thought into their speech, though here the subcurrent of thought is ostensibly verbalized _as it occurs_. The dual status of such utterances has been discussed by Goffman. Using them, the speaker "renders readily accessible to witnesses what he chooses to assign to his inward state" (Goffman 1978:794). Muttering is much the same (ibid. 796).

There is of course also mental activity involved in the routine processing of speech. Beyond the automatic and largely unconscious cognitive processing involved in basic speech production and comprehension, we draw inferences, devise and notice implicatures, reconstruct the targets of speech errors, distinguish given and new, recover material elided in ritualized encoun-

ters, take note of lurking presuppositions, identify
denigrations, and marshal various other monitorings and
pragmatic operations the extent of which is apt to be
grossly underestimated if one looks only at solitary,
unsituated sentences.

What we call speakers are also thinkers, with one
foot in the interactive world of their talk and other
behavior, and the other in an internal world of mental
proceedings, which they may, or not, choose to express.

The inaccessibility of covert thinking to the researcher is what has sometimes been called the problem
of 'intention', 'meaning', or 'motivation' (see Duncan
and Fiske 1977:17). Students of conversation are for
the most part[3] limited to working with what is said or
done rather than what is thought, and to the extent that
conversants themselves find each other's thoughts indis-
cernible, it has seemed both necessary and fair to researchers to restrict their attention to what is audibly
and, if video equipment is used, visibly expressed.
It nevertheless remains true that there is thought 'beneath' the speech and other overt behavior of participants in a conversation, and that the course of their
thoughts may not be entirely synchronous or identical
to the course of their talk, let alone fully accessible
to even the most talented of researchers.

The bias toward what is manifest is often simply
adopted as a methodological principle (e.g. Duncan and
Fiske 1977:17); or, as in the work of Sacks, Schegloff,
and others, may be taken to define the range of phenomena
under investigation:

> Our analysis has sought to explicate the ways in
> which the materials are produced by members in order-
> ly ways that exhibit their orderliness, have their
> orderliness appreciated and used, and have that

appreciation displayed and treated as the basis for subsequent action (Schegloff and Sacks 1973:290).

Even in conversational analyses supposedly limited to 'observables', however, the researcher must often engage in guesswork. Studies of this kind are peppered with qualifiers necessary because what is displayed by conversants permits multiple interactional interpretations all consistent with their talk.

What is unmanifested is not entirely excludable from the analysis of conversation, then, but neither--practically speaking--can it be fully included. The middle ground, though an unsettled one, is to acknowledge the existence and importance of unexpressed thinking to what is said and done by conversants, and also to acknowledge its inaccessibility to direct observation. This tempered point of view seems to characterize much of the work of Garfinkel and Goffman (see, esp., Garfinkel 1972).

1.3 Three 'Worlds' of the Speaker

Though some conversation analysts may, for practical reasons, exclude covert thinking from consideration, speakers do not. To describe the position of the individual participant in a conversation, a tripartite model seems essential. The covert thinking of the speaker, what that speaker has presently in mind but has not disclosed will be referred to below as the _private world_; what is on display as talk and other behavior on the part of conversants and is thus available to both the speaker and any other(s) will be called the _shared world_; and the covert thinking of other conversants, which is inaccessible to the speaker, will be called the _other world_. This terminology is applicable equally to any of the participants in a conversation, so that what is private world for one conversant may, for another, be other world.

That conversants should be described as orienting to the existence of these three different spheres of activity is certainly not a revolutionary claim, though it seems that conversants are not often conceived of in this way and are more often simply viewed as manufacturers of audible, recordable talk.[4]

There will be repeated occasion in later chapters to refer to the tripartite model of the speaker's world just proposed. The disclosure problem discussed above, which will be the basis for understanding items such as like, well, and you know, can be restated in the context of this model as follows:

> The Disclosure Problem: Current undisclosed material in the private and other worlds may be communicatively relevant to what the speaker is now doing, or has just now done, or will just now be doing, in the shared world.[5]

In the discussion that follows it will be helpful to keep in mind that the 'contents' of the shared world differ in some important respects from those of the two covert worlds. Material spoken into the shared world may be strategically placed there and is subject to what Sacks et al. have called recipient design:

> a multitude of respects in which the talk by a party in a conversation is constructed or designed in ways which display an orientation and sensitivity to the particular other(s) who are the co-participants (1974:727).

Moreover, speakers are constrained by the sequential requirements of conversation. Answers, to take a well-worked example, are contingent upon questions; or, more precisely, what follows a question should be placed there with sensitivity to the conditioned relevance of an answer at that point (cf. Goffman 1976). The recent literature on conversational repair, to take a second example, illustrates the strategic nature of some contributions of talk. Speakers regularly fail to initiate repair on another's repairable utterance until it becomes obvious that the repairable will not be self-corrected by its speaker (Schegloff et al., 1977). On other occasions participants choose not to initiate repair on some obviously repairable item (Schegloff et al. 1977:375 refer to these occasions as 'opportunities NOT TAKEN'), possibly because the repair, which would involve work by both parties, doesn't seem worth the trouble, or might implicate disagreement. In these situations--delayed repair and intentional non-repair--it appears that thinking is left temporarily unexpressed in the first case, and altogether unexpressed in the second.

The shared world, then, is in general one in which what is placed there is to some serviceable degree intendedly understandable by interlocutors based on their shared knowledge, including knowledge of what has earlier, and just, been said and done by them in the conversation.

In contrast--though here there are only difficult introspections to guide us--unexpressed thought seems not to respect sequential and politeness conventions governing talk by well-behaved conversants, and in principle needn't be explicit, complete, or well-formed, since it is not necessarily designed or destined for presentation in the shared world. The situation in the covert worlds would appear to be altogether less constrained than is external behavior. 'Free' associations are certainly possible; thoughts may be tangential to the present line of conversation or even quite unrelated to it. Talk and thought, though occurring in the same speaking situation, need not run parallel. It may even be

inappropriate to speak of 'the course of thinking' as
if it possessed a cohesiveness and structural integrity
similar to what appears in discourse. It would be pre-
ferable to use a very general term like 'state of consciousness' (Keller 1981) or 'internal state' (Lakoff
1974) to refer to covert thinking rather than suggest,
as in Goldberg (1976:39) that covert thinking constitutes
a separate unspoken conversation concurrent with what
is actually said, or that what appears as talk is simply
a selection from such an internal conversation or mono-
logue.[6]

1.4 Routinization

In any discussion of discourse particles, the question of routinization arises constantly. Many such items
have come to be so closely associated with particular
discourse situations that they may be considered conventional responses to these situations. For example, _well_,
with low-rising intonation, is a conventional response
to the situation in which one conversant awaits an over-
due response from another. _Well_, used in this way, may
therefore be considered a _routine_ (see Coulmas 1980).
Routines are "highly conventionalized pre-patterned expressions (or single words) whose occurrence is tied
to more or less standardized communication situations"
(ibid., 3). The meaning of items of verbal routine is
thought to differ from that of other, nonroutine items
in that the literal meaning may be outshown, oversha-
dowed, or even altogether obscured by the conventional
use of the item, or the conventional use may be taken
to characterize the item to the total exclusion of any
literal meaning. The routine _goodbye_, for example (see
Clark and French 1981; cf. Laver 1981), occurs in a specifiable discourse situation (leave taking) and constitutes

a conventionalized response to this situation, but if we ask the meaning of the item, informants balk. Either we must admit that the item _has_ no particular meaning, or broaden the concept of meaning to include conventional use, which is, in effect, what lexicographers do with such items. _Webster's Collegiate_ (1979) lists only the following brief 'definition' for _good-bye_: "a concluding remark or gesture at parting".

Good-bye is a special example in two respects: it has a single predominant routine use, and it has no discernible literal meaning. Neither of these features can be extended to routines in general. Often a single item has multiple uses, and often indeed a routine does have some specifiable literal meaning. The speaker who repeatedly issues the word _right_ while listening to a complex argument may well have a literal meaning of the item ('correct') in mind despite using the word as a point-granting routine. It is unlikely that such routines as _how are you?_, _take care_, and _see you_ are entirely devoid of literal meaning. _See you_, like _good-bye_, is used for leave taking, but, consonant with its literal reading, is appropriate for temporary rather than permanent leave taking. _How are you?_ despite its basically phatic use (cf. Malinowski 1946:248-251) can elicit a response relevant to its literal meaning.

It would be a mistake, though, to insist too strongly on the literal meaning of routines. It is perfectly possible that on specific occasions of utterance their literal meaning is more or less disregarded in favor of their routine function. The sometimes lax attention paid to the literal meaning of routines is exemplified by the peculiar item _I could care less_ (Tannen and Öztek 1981) which sometimes replaces _I couldn't care less_. Tannen and Öztek claim that the interchangeability of these two items illustrates the purely conventional nature of the expressions and their loss of all contact with literal meaning. But the literal meaning is not really so far away. For one thing, _less_ is a negative item which, under the less attentive conditions under which routines tend to be uttered, might itself be felt by the speaker to convey the missing sentential negation (note that comparatives in general seem to involve an internal negation; thus they occur with negative polarity items: _less than anyone_); for another thing, it is difficult to imagine this expression--with its present use--evolving at any future point into, for example _I couldn't care more_, _I could say less_, or _I must care less_; notice also that the occurrence of this item in construction (_I could care less about your old shoe_) speaks quite strongly for the retention of literal meaning.

In the discussion of _like_, _well_ and _y(ou) know_ in the following chapters, it will be necessary to keep in mind both the likelihood of their routinization with different functions and the compatability of this routinization with each item's having a basic or core use which might remain constant through all the routine functions of the item. The watchword 'routine' should not be taken as a license to forget the basic linguistic value, if any, of an item, although this value, if there is one, might be less than fully present in the mind of the speaker on a given occasion of utterance. This notion seems to be implicit in the following claim by Coulmas:

> Every normal member of a speech community can distinguish routine utterances from idiosyncratic ones. Furthermore, he knows that routine usage affects the meaningfulness of expressions, and he knows whether or not an utterance is to be _assigned the full force of its literal meaning_ (1981:16; emphasis mine).

As Coulmas notes, the degree of meaningfulness of

an item may depend to an extent on its frequency of occur
rence. The more an item is used routinely, the more
it is apt to lose contact with its literal meaning, an
idea commemorated in the phrase 'crying wolf'. In the
case of the discourse particles under study here, the
question is more appropriately formulated as one of use
rather than meaning, but the general point still holds.
The position to be taken below is that the basic use
of each discourse particle discussed can be dominated
by its specific routine functions, but is never completely obliterated, remains available to scrutiny, and, most
importantly, defines the possibilities for the multiple
routine uses of the item. This position is first developed and exemplified in Chapter 3 with the item _like_.

1.5 Use of Speech Materials

Several types of data were used for this study.
Materials designated RTS below are from tape recordings
of radio talk show conversations. Callers engage the
show's host in a brief discussion related to the chosen
topic for that evening, or the host engages a celebrity
'guest caller' in conversation. Two important features
of these materials are that kinesics play no role since
the callers and the host cannot see each other, and that
the recordings themselves are free of any possible in-
vestigative bias because there is no personal contact
between the investigator and either callers or host.[7]
Materials designated LAB consist of three extended
dyadic face-to-face conversations between friends (3
pairs, 6 speakers total). Pairs of friends were chosen
to create as relaxed a situation as possible. The subjects were seated in comfortable chairs a few feet apart
and were allowed to talk about whatever they wished.
Neither the tape recorder nor the researcher were present

in the room where the conversations took place, though microphones were present and visible. Judging by the intimate nature of some of the topics discussed, the LAB conversants were probably not much intimidated by the recording situation.[8] All six speakers were undergraduate student volunteers; all were native residents of central Ohio. The only selection criterion was the pre-existing friendship of the members of each pair.

In some cases below part of an analysis will be based on intuitive judgments of acceptability, but because of the well-known problems in interpreting such data, wherever feasible important points will be illustrated with several observed examples. In some cases, statistical evaluations of distribution will be presented.

Examples cited in the text appear in different 'reader's' transcription systems, according to the source of the data. Examples taken from published work by other researchers (with one exception noted in Chapter 4) appear in the transcription system used in the quoted source. Examples drawn from RTS and LAB materials appear in a reader's notation similar to that used in Schenkein (1978), but with a few modifications. Symbols appearing in all examples are explained in the List of Symbols. Reader's transcription is intended to make a conversation readily accessible to the reader's eye. No attempt is made to render fine phonetic detail or to specify the relative timing of items with great accuracy.[9] Such transcript notations naturally embody numerous claims about what is significant in an excerpted stretch of talk and should not be taken to represent a complete or utterly objective rendering of any conversation. Such transcripts do, however, strive for the inclusion of all and only those vocal sounds occurring in a conversation, and they do purport to accurately indicate the identity of the speaker responsible for each particular contribution of talk. The transcription systems in widest use also permit the transcriber to indicate uncertainty with regard to materials that are partially audible or otherwise problematic.

The limited use in this study of statistical analyses of large numbers of instances of the items under study has proved successful enough to suggest the general usefulness of this type of data in the analysis of conversation structure. The general objection to quantitative analyses of individual conversational items (voiced, for example, in Schegloff 1981) is that the items cannot be productively extracted from their individual situations of utterance--that is, that they cannot be fully appreciated without examining their position in the extended, sequentially organized body of talk of which they are parts. This objection to the use of quantitative analysis is ill-founded insofar as it assumes that discourse items are to be entirely understood in terms of their role in particular conversational contexts. The analysis to be proposed below will be attentive to the possibility that such items may have a specifiable linguistic use which may partly govern their distribution with respect to adjacent linguistic items and structures. It seems very likely that the entire area of conversational studies can benefit from a more quantitative approach. It is almost always possible to test the conclusions derived from micro-sequential analyses of the sort done by Schegloff, Jefferson and others by statistically examining distributional predictions based on these conclusions. An admirably clear and valuable example is provided by Clark and French (1981).

1.6 Outline of Remaining Chapters

In Chapter 2 a class of items referred to as _evin-_

cives is characterized; these are lexical items the primary function of which is to exhibit the existence of unexpressed thinking at a particular moment of utterance without displaying this thinking in detail. Most of the items discussed in later chapters are evincives in this sense. As an illustration of the evincive nature of items such as _well_ and _oh_, their function in one particular discourse context, quotation, is discussed at length.

Chapters 3, 4, and 5 discuss particular discourse items (_like_, _well_ and _you know_, respectively) whose basic use is related to the disclosure problem. _Like_ and _well_ are evincives, but _you know_, while similar to ordinary evincives in some respects, is related to the disclosure problem in a different way.

Chapter 6 contains general remarks on _like_, _well_ and _you know_ and discusses implications of the proposed treatment for theories of conversational behavior. These three items are related to others, including _now_, _I mean_, _mind you_, and several items most commonly referred to as interjections. These items are compared to each other in relation to the tripartite model of the speaker's view proposed in 1.3 above and to the general problem of disclosure that is statable in terms of that model. A useful framework emerges that could be used to compare ways in which the disclosure problem is handled in different languages.

CHAPTER TWO

EVINCIVES

2.1 Interjections as Evincives

According to James (1974:1-5), traditional descriptions of interjections usually mention two definitive characteristics: (1) such forms express some strong emotion on the part of the speaker, and (2) they bear no clear grammatical relationship to other elements in the sentences in which they occur. The concern of this chapter is with the first of these putative characteristics. The claim that emotion is what is involved with these items will be re-examined and a reformulation proposed that captures their relation to disclosure (See 1.3).

While it is true that interjections are usually viewed as grammatically independent expressions of strong emotion--and this seems patently true of such items as ouch--traditional descriptions mention other features of this class as well. Jespersen, for example, offers this definition: "interjections are abrupt expressions for sudden sensations and emotions" (1923:415); and Fries describes interjections as "spontaneous reactions to situations suddenly confronting the speaker (1952: fn26). Based on these quotations from Jespersen and Fries, a third component of the traditional definition of interjections can be identified. This feature is hinted at in their words "abrupt", "sudden", and "spontaneous": interjections are somehow tied to the speaker's present internal state, or to use the terminology proposed in Chapter 1, these quotations suggest that interjections are reflections of the private world.

A fourth possible component of the definition emerges in a further claim by Fries (1952:53) that the

- 17 -

meanings of interjections are to be "inferred from the situations in which they usually occur". Although James (1972) has argued that some interjections do have a particular meaning that persists regardless of context, it will be claimed below that there is nonetheless some truth to what Fries says. While many interjections do have a specifiable meaning, part of their meaning is dependent in an interesting way on interpretation in context.

The idea that what is expressed by interjections is "strong emotion" is incorrect. James (1974) noticed that some interjections, such as _oh_ (in some uses to be discussed below) and _well_, do not seem to express strong emotion. It will be argued below that a generalization that does characterize a large number of items traditionally called interjections is that they indicate some form of unexpressed thinking on the part of the speaker.

The claims that interjections indicate unexpressed thinking, that they are somehow abrupt or spontaneous in that they reflect the current speaker's present internal state, and that they are subject to a certain amount of contextual interpretation while nevertheless having a specifiable core use, can be captured by considering interjections to be _evincives_, where this term is defined as follows:

> EVINCIVE[1]: a linguistic item that indicates that at the moment at which it is said the speaker is engaged in, or has just then been engaged in, thinking; the evincive item indicates that this thinking is now occurring or has just now occurred but does not completely specify its content.

According to the definition to just proposed, evincives are tied to the moment of utterance. This important point deserves elaboration. Items like _aha_ are

not simply expressions of the existence of undisclosed
thought but express something about the current contents
of the private world. There is no occasion (aside from
mention) on which this item can be used other than as
a direct reflection of the speaker's state of mind at
the moment of utterance. Even if the item is attributed
to someone in a quotation,

(1) John said, "Aha, the century plant bloomed".

it is understood to reflect the current state of the
quoted speaker's mind at the retrospectively quoted
moment of utterance. In this way items like aha differ
from ordinary lexical items, which are not tied to the
current or quoted moment of utterance. While ordinary
verbs, adjectives, and so on may mask undisclosed thinking, it is not their specific function to do so, and
they do not indicate current undisclosed thinking.

The term evincive is chosen here rather than interjection so that the term used for these items will adequately reflect the fact that some of what is mentioned
or 'brought up' by using such items remains in the private world. Evincives are flags marking the presence
of unspoken thought.[2] This feature of evincives will
become clear in the following discussion of particular
items, and also underlies the discussion in later chapters.

The distinction between interjections and discourse
particles or markers has been lost in the foregoing
discussion. This merger was intentional. There is
already an overlap between items that go by these different names. James, for example, refers to well and
now as interjections, while the same items are considered discourse particles or markers by Goldberg (1980)
and Schiffrin (1981a). It should be emphasized, though,
that the intention here in using the term evincive is

not only to avoid the terminological problem, but to clarify the basic nature of certain items whose status as evincives is, I would like to claim, more basic than either their membership in the traditional word class interjections or their more specific roles in structuring discourse.

The evincive items in linguistic systems enable speakers to express the importance of what they have in mind at a particular point in a conversation, without fully displaying their thinking. For example, the evincive well, as will be argued at length in Chapter 4, indicates that the speaker, at the point at which the item is uttered, is consulting his or her then present thoughts, but does not specify the exact nature of these thoughts. The need for evincives such as well arises primarily from a general restriction on conversational behavior formulated in one clause of Grice's Maxim of Quantity: "Do not make your contribution more informative than is required" (Grice 1977:45)[3]. It is often relevant for a speaker to bring up that something is in mind, but not to bring up exactly what is in mind. For example, the speaker issuing well before a considered reply to a question refrains from displaying for interlocutors all the unessential details of the ruminations that lead to the answer; to mention the details might implicate, possibly to the detriment of communication, that these details are viewed by the speaker as significant enough to deserve mention.

Because they are tied to the moment of utterance, evincives have an added virtue: they enable speakers to establish the timeliness of what they have in mind with respect to the measured delivery of their utterances. Thus the use of an item like ah in conversation establishes that the moment of utterance (of ah) corresponds to the occurrence of some covert mental event (ah is discussed further below); that is, it establishes the real time locus of some mentionable covert mental event that may come up in the shared world only later in the conversation. Consider the following hypothetical exchange:

> (2) A: There were four concerts today, all in the evening.
> B: Ah! That explains why Chris didn't come to the meeting: she must have been asked to work on one of the sound crews.

This use of ah marks as occurring after A's word evening a mental event of B's which is then delineated by B's ensuing talk. Time elapses during the explanation of B's covert thinking, but through the use of ah, the under-lying thought itself is marked as occurring at precisely the relevant spot. Evincives are therefore of obvious use in establishing the speaker's accountability. To say

> (3) I didn't make the phone call you asked me to.

can be quite different from saying

> (4) Oh! I didn't make the phone call you asked me to.

since oh in (4) can be used to indicate that a thought expressed in the sentence following oh just entered the speaker's mind and thereby implicate that the speaker's failure to make the call was due to forgetfulness, not malevolent intent.

Evincives as a class are therefore capable of two general and important functions in conversation: most fundamentally, they establish the conversational rele-vance--but not the details--of undisclosed thinking by the speaker; and they can mark the real time moment of occurrence of that thinking in order to establish the timeliness of a speaker's reaction. These items thus respond to the disclosure problem by addressing the incongruity of the unrestricted flow of mental events in the private world and the restricted flow of talk in the shared world. Section 2.2 will examine the way in which these two related properties of evincives can be used to explain their function in directly reported speech.

2.2 Evincives in Quotations

To illustrate the role of evincives, it is instructive to examine their use in a particular conversational situation in which they occur with great frequency. An examination of the speech materials used for this study revealed that large numbers of evincive items occur as the first item in direct quotations, as in these fabricated examples:

(5) Robert said, "Well, posture is important."
(6) Ann said, "Oh, I don't think Malthus was an American".

2.2.1 Well and Oh in Quotations

A corpus of 328 conversational quotations was assembled from the RTS and LAB materials and several published data sources (in Sudnow 1972, Schenkein 1978, Chafe 1980, and Schiffrin 1981a). All clear instances of quotation in each source were included. In this corpus well and oh occur quite frequently in quotation-initial position. These two items begin 74 of the 328 quotations (22.6%; cf. Table 1 below).

Well is in general found in conversation more at the beginnings of speaking turns than in other positions. Svartvik (1980:169), for example, remarks that half of the well's in a large corpus of British English conversation he studied were turn-initial; the other half were distributed between various other positions. Surveying one 8,000 word LAB conversaton, 50 well's were found,

TABLE 1

Turn & Quote Initial _Well_ & _Oh_ in a Conversation
of 336 Turns Including 62 Turn Internal Quotations

	Oh	Well	Combined
Turn Initial	12	23	35
Quote Initial	9	10	19

Chi-square (df=1):

oh: 10.46 (p<0.01)
Well: 5.94 (p<0.02)
combined: 16.59 (p<0.001)

TABLE 2

111 Quote Initial Interjections in a Corpus of 328
Conversational Quotations

well	(47)	whoa	(1)
oh	(27)	shh	(1)
hey	(7)	hhh	(1)
man	(3)	wow	(1)
aha	(2)	tsk	(1)
hmm	(2)	howdy	(1)
um	(2)	(bz::)	(1)
hi	(2)	(uno)	(1)
(i::)	(2)	poof	(1)
mmm	(1)	(hæ)	(1)
ah	(1)	HHOHHhhh	(1)
eh	(1)	uuoo-ooo-ooo	(1)
hah	(1)		

of which 23 (46%) are turn-initial[4], a figure comparable
to Svartvik's estimate. Of the remaining 27 well's,
10 are quotation-initial. As shown in Table 1, well
is significantly more likely to occur initial in a turn-
internal quotation than in turn-initial position, the
position in which well occurs most frequently overall.
The situation is essentially the same for oh: there is
again a significant disparity between the two positions
in the direction of there being more instances of the
item beginning quotes than speaking turns.

When quotation-initial items are examined in general, many apparently evincive items are found in the same
position. Table 2 is a list of the interjections occurring in quotation-initial position (including all items
not obviously belonging, in their present use, to some
'sentential' word class). As apparent from this table,
just over a third of the quotations begin with an interjection (34%). The usual rate of occurrence of initial
interjections, based on LAB-A turn beginnings, is 13%
(44/337). The overall difference is significant at
$p < .001$ (chi-square 40.18; df=1).

Some explanation is required for the preponderance
of interjections in quotation-initial position as opposed
to other discourse positions. This skew distribution
is counterintuitive on the assumption that quotations
are direct reports of actually occurring talk.[5] If quotations are factual reports, the incidence of initial interjections in quotations should be no higher than in un-
quoted utterances. But the assumption that quotations
are factual reports is in fact unwarranted. There is
much evidence that quotation could not be literal. This
is clear from numerous experiments in which neither short-
nor long-term memory has proved accessible for strictly
verbatim detail when there has been no attempt at verba-

tim memorization (see Sachs 1967, Wanner 1974). Moreover, speakers seem to have a tacit understanding of their limitations in this regard and permit each other to present as directly quoted material differing unimportantly from what may have actually been said; a plausible equivalent can pass as a direct quotation.

Since in casual talk no one expects quotations to be exact, ordinarily B's response in (7) would be heard as unduly stringent:

(7) A: ... so I asked Harvey for the time, and he said, "Around four thirty".
     B: I was there at the time, and what he really said was, "About half past four".

In fact, when speakers quote verbatim, they tend, if it matters, to mark what they say accordingly:

(8) Eve said, and these are her exact words, "Bugaku sickens me".

Since quoted speech is partly constructed anyway, the occurrence of more initial interjections within quotations than occur outside of them is not paradoxical. It must be that speakers _insert_ these items when they construct quotations. The question that then remains is _why_ they do so.

Here it is helpful to enlist the features of evincives mentioned in the previous section. One feature of these items is that they establish the existence of the speaker's undisclosed thought without displaying it in detail. This aspect of evincives makes them potentially quite useful in contextualizing quotations, which, as pieces of nonpresent situations, stand in particular need of such contextualization. Evincives situate the quotation and the quoted speaker by portraying that speaker as 'with thought' and specifying the general quality or cast of the speaker's thought at that point. It is to the reporting speaker's advantage to prepare the ground on which a quotation can have its desired force by establishing the quoted speaker as present in and mindful of the (recalled or imagined) proceedings - as integral, that is, to the situation from which the quotation is drawn. By using particular evincives, the quoting speaker can do this easily in a number of specifiably different ways. The most popular choices by far are <u>well</u> and <u>oh</u>, though they are simply the most statistically prominent members of a fairly large class of items the function of which is to mediate between undisclosed thinking and overt behavior. Using these forms, speakers can, at a single stroke, bring the tenor of their thoughts and the fact that they are, or have just been, thinking, into play in the conversation, without exhibiting unnecessary detail. This function of evincives will be referred to as <u>backgrounding</u>.

As a backgrounder, <u>well</u> (see Chapter 4) indicates that the speaker is 'with' mental contents at the moment of uttering <u>well</u>, or, more specifically, that the speaker is consulting these mental contents. The discussion of <u>oh</u>, the second most frequently occurring item in Table 2, must take into account at least two distinct items designated by James oh_1 and oh_2. Oh_1, according to James, indicates that the speaker has just become aware of something--a piece of information, a sudden strong emotion, or that s/he should perform some speech act (James 1974:37). Oh_2 indicates that the speaker has paused to make a decision or choice between alternatives, none of which is the correct, right, or accurate one (<u>ibid.</u>, 84); because it means this, oh_2 also tends to express casualness. Examples of oh_1 and oh_2 appear in (9) and (10).

(9) Oh! What a lovely drill press!

(10) Sander would probably go for, oh, a nice bordeaux.

Oh_1 is clearly evincive: it indicates that some thought has just now occurred but does not, itself, express what the thought is. Oh_2, also evincive, indicates that alternatives are under consideration but does not specify them. Typically, but not always, oh_1 is followed by an explanation; oh_2 normally is not.

James notes that oh_1 can occur in response to a statement; it then indicates that the speaker did not know the information in the statement:

(11) A: ...So this argument proves that Quantifier-Float is global.
B: Oh.   (James 1974:28)

Here the evincive function of oh is preempted by A's statement--what oh evinces precedes it in plain view.

James mentions a third use of oh (hereafter oh_3) which she claims is close to oh_2 but seems to indicate only casualness:

(12) A: There sure aren't very many people here.
B: Oh, more people will probably come.
                                      (James 1974:25)

Oh_3, though more casual, is very similar in use to well and thus also appears to be evincive.

The use of oh in quotations usually involves oh_1, though at times it is hard to distinguish oh_1 from oh_3. The backgrounding function of oh_1 is to provide that the speaker has just noticed something; it thereby establishes the speaker as present and mindfully reacting in the situation of the quoted utterance. Both well and oh are tied to the particular present moment of utterance of the quoted speaker. Because of this, their use has the effect of invoking or 'creating' the moment at which the utterance occurred, and so providing a 'living' context for the quote. Because forms like _well_ and _oh_ are reflections of the private world, they establish the existence of that world with respect to the quoted speaker and thus portray that speaker as someone with mental contents contributing in an ordinary way to the shared world and also engaging in undisclosed thinking. The claim, then, is that the occurrence of so many evincives in quotation-initial position is due to their insertion there by quoting speakers as a routine part of the process of constructing quotations: such items are optional but are frequently inserted quotation-initially because they background the quotation enhancing the usefulness of the quotation to the quoting speaker's communicative purpose.

Many of the other items in Table 2 are also evincive, and so serve the same function, but each in a slightly different way. The summons _hey_, often found preceding a vocative, is the third most frequent item in Table 2. Summonses seek attention but also indicate having in mind something to say or do:

(13) Hey! Hand me that socket wrench.

The summons itself does not present thoughts but evinces them as covertly there. For this reason a felicitous summons precedes some indication, linguistic or otherwise, of the speaker's intention in issuing it. Beginning a quotation, _hey_ specifies that the quoted speaker wished to make a contribution. Because it is a summons, _hey_ marks the quotation as directed to some other(s) and situated as part, possibly the first part, of some ordinary proceeding in which speakers oriented to each other in a manner routine for conversations. _Hey_, like _well_ and _oh_, then, backgrounds--it provides context for appreciating the ensuing quotation; specifically, it tells us something about the quoted speaker's 'state of consciousness' (cf. use of this term in Keller 1981).

Aha occurs twice quotation-initially. In the present data aha indicates that the speaker now sees a connection previously missed or has pieced together the logic of a situation. Aha evinces that some connection has just now been made, without itself specifying either what the connection is or by what mental process the speaker arrived at it.

Ah has a different use. According to James (1974: 37), it indicates that the speaker has just now thought of something and finds that thing, or having thought of it, pleasing or significant. Ah and aha differ in use:

(14) We went down to ... ah! Spindrift Beach on
      the Fourth.
(15) We went down to ... aha! Spindrift Beach on
      the Fourth.

(14) could be said if the speaker is pleased to have remembered the name of the beach, but (15) cannot, I think, have this meaning and would most likely be taken to imply--oddly--that the speaker has only just now deduced the name of the beach. Both ah and aha are evincive but differ in what they attribute to the undisclosed thinking of the speaker.

Man, often a term of address, also has an evincive use:

(16) Man! Is this chili ever hot!

As an evincive, man! indicates that a speaker finds what s/he has in mind at that point amazing or at least mildly surprising. Compare:

(17) Man! A comet just hit Randy.
(18) Man! You can't store water in a sieve.

Anyone saying (18) might be seen as slow-witted. Another

item in Table 2, <u>wow</u>, seems quite similar in use to evincive <u>man</u>.

Filled pause is represented in Table 2 by two instances of <u>um</u>. Both <u>um</u> and <u>uh</u> evince mental contents that are momentarily null, indistinct, or unresolvable, and as such have many uses in conversation. <u>Well</u>, in contrast, indicates more pointed deliberation or consideration. Compare (19) and (20) as answers to the questions, "What are you doing over the Fourth?"

(19)   Well, I don't know.
(20)   Uh, I don't know.

<u>Hmm</u> and <u>mmm</u>, with sharply falling intonation, can mark conclusive appreciation or consideration; the meaning of these items varies widely, depending on intonation.

A few items in Table 2 (e.g. [i::]) are probably occasional inventions (some of them written in the published eye-dialect renderings of their transcribers), but seem to be evincive. Two items are not evincive: <u>hi</u> and <u>howdy</u>. These greeting words do not mark the occurrence of undisclosed thinking. One may, of course, think privately while uttering such a greeting word, but the word itself does not indicate this.

2.3   Enquoting

It is thus possible to explain the inordinate frequency of occurrence of evincives initial in quotations by considering their usefulness as backgrounders in connection with the need of quotations for the kind of backgrounding they provide. Another factor may well be involved in the skew distribution of evincive items in quotations, though this second factor is probably less important than the backgrounding function.

Both *well* and *oh* are found almost exclusively in utterance-initial position. In her work based on introspective data James has made much of the fact that both items can occur sentence-internally, as in

(21) There were, well, four of them.
(22) There were, oh, four of them.

but in fact this use of these forms is statistically unusual. All 110 instances of *well* and *oh* in LAB materials used for this study, for example, are initial. Sentences like (21) and (22) no doubt occur, but not very often.

Since *well* and *oh* predominantly occur initially, they may cue initiation, and if so, a second reason for the unexpectedly high frequency of evincives in quotation-initial position suggests itself: perhaps quotation-initial evincives mark the quotation as a 'beginning'. Since most quotations occur within a matrix sentence, issuing an initiator within a sentence, particularly after a verb of saying, may cue a beginning within the utterance unit, which is one way of describing a turn-internal quotation (the speaker does, in effect, change[6]).

2.4 Quotation

To quote, speakers must indicate that after a certain point what they say is to be understood as quoted and face an opposite task when the quotation is done: how to signal a return to present contributions of talk, from the citation of prior talk, possible talk, or projected future talk. The first task will be called *enquoting*; the other one, *unquoting*, will be ignored in what follows.

A primary resource for quotation is introduction of quoted material with a verb of verbal communication, usually, *say*:

(23)   Theresa said, "David, just go".

But use of these verbs doesn't itself enquote, as shown by spoken sentences ambiguous between a direct and an indirect reading:[7]

(24)   Theresa said David just left for Ontario.
(25)   Asa said I'm to blame.

Since such sentences are on one reading paraphrasable by ones like (26) and (27),

(26)   Theresa said that David just left for Ontario.
(27)   Asa said that I'm to blame.

enquoting is not accomplished simply by saying (24) or (25).   Failure to enquote can lead to misunderstandings: for example, (25) leaves it unclear whether Asa or the speaker of (25) is considered to blame.   Narrative <u>go</u>, as in (28) does enquote (Schourup 1982):

(28)   Mort goes, "We should leave."
(29)   *Mort goes that we should leave.

but speakers who avoid <u>go</u> 'say', as most over thirty seem to (Butters 1980), cannot in general enquote by the choice of a verb alone.

There are, however, other resources available for enquoting involving the quoted material itself.   Enquoting occurs when the quoted material exhibits one or more features peculiar to directly reported speech (a list of these appears in Banfield 1973).   Thus, for example, WH-questions after <u>said</u> are heard as directly quoted:

(30)   Muriel said, "Who are you?"
(31)   *Muriel said that who are you?

To enquote, speakers could select for quotation material that will be unambiguously heard as directly reported.

Or speakers might <u>enlist</u> features of directly reported speech to enquote, refashioning what they wish to quote to make it sound more direct.   Possibly speakers

insert items such as well and oh quotation-initially
to enquote. That they might do so is suggested by the
fact that insertion of an evincive does enquote:

(32) Lyle said steak would be fine.
(33) Lyle said oh steak would be fine.

While (32) is ambiguous between a direct and an indirect
reading, (33) is only capable of the direct reading.

This interpretation of well and oh as enquoting
initiators marches well with a curious fact for which
there is otherwise no apparent explanation. Consider
spoken sentences capable of two readings, one in which
the interjection is quotation-initial, and one in which
it is the last item before the quotation begins:

(34) John said well plastics are the future.
(35) Marla said oh Grace takes Chemistry 103.

Subjects strongly tend to assign the interjection to
the quoted speaker, not the quoting one, even though
the interjection could reasonably be attributed to the
quoting speaker, as would occur when what follows the
interjection is an indirect report:

(36) John said, well, that plastics are the future.
(37) Marla said, oh, that Grace takes Chemistry
     103.

A simple experiment was done to test this point. Sentences (34) and (35) were presented in written form without punctuation or capitalization and subjects were asked
to punctuate them. Table 3 shows the result. Most subjects added quotation marks before the interjections.

TABLE 3

Quote-Allegiance of Well and Oh

	Well	Oh
Assigned to quoted speaker	51	56
Assigned to quoting speaker	2	0
Uninterpretable response	_5	_2
	58	58

Another group of subjects was asked to punctuate the
same sentences without the interjections. Only half
of these (12/24) used quotation marks. Considered in
conjunction with Table 3, this datum suggests that well
and oh could serve an important enquoting function in
addition to serving as backgrounders.

Whether speakers do heavily depend on well and oh,
and other evincives for enquoting is, however, subject
to some question. In many cases a quotation begun with
an evincive is introduced with go 'say', so that the
enquoting is already performed before the evincive is
issued:

> (38) ... and she goes "Well if my check's big enough
> I'll buy ya an eight- or a twelve pack ...
> (LAB-A,9)
> (39) ... and he's just goin(g) "Oh come on hurry
> up" (LAB-A,16)

Probably the enquoting function of evincives should not
be dismissed entirely. It is certainly true that forms
like well and oh are capable of this function (as seen
in Table 3), but examples like (38) and (39) suggest
that their role in enquoting is not always crucial.[8]

The backgrounding function of evincives is logically

prior to their enquoting function. It is the capability of evincives to initiate utterances that makes them suitable for enquoting, but their tendency to occur initially is itself due to the fact that they are backgrounders: it is natural that evincives strongly tend to occur in initial position, since this is rhetorically the natural place for backgrounding material to appear. In quotations, for example, the speaker will wish to <u>first</u> establish the quoted speaker as present in the situation of the quoted utterance, rather than belatedly attempt to background the quotation after it is under way.

The enquoting function is discussed further in Chapter 4 in connection with the discourse functions of <u>well</u>.

2.5 Summary

The notion 'evincive' is applicable to a number of items occurring in ordinary conversation. Many forms usually described as interjections are evincive in function. The backgrounding function of many evincives makes them useful in quotation. Backgrounding is not a function only of quoted evincives, but the usefulness of evincives to background quotations is great because quotations, as excerpts from non-present situations, stand in need of contextualization. It is not surprising, therefore, that evincives occur more frequently initial in quotations than initial in speaking turns. In that position evincives may, additionally, serve an enquoting function owing to their particular suitability for initiation.

Evincives represent one kind of speaker response to the problem of disclosure discussed in Chapter 1. Specifically, evincives like <u>well</u> and <u>oh</u> allow the speaker to call attention to current thought in the private world and to specify, with a broad stroke, the tenor

of what is in mind, without placing the details of the
speaker's thoughts in the shared world. Using evincives,
the speaker may acknowledge the existence and importance
of the private world to current conversational behavior
and so solve that part of the disclosure problem that
relates to the private world.

CHAPTER THREE

LIKE

3.1 Like in Conversation

The concern of this chapter is conventional uses of like beyond those regularly attested as standard in dictionaries. The received uses of like mentioned in Webster's Third New International Dictionary are:

1. as a transitive verb:

   I'd like to have my back rubbed.

2. as a noun:

   Everyone has likes and dislikes.
   the like(s) of which the world has never known

3. as an adjective with various meanings, including 'the same or nearly so' and 'likely':

   tables of like color
   dishes that are like to please you

4. as a preposition with numerous meanings, including 'similar to', 'typical of', 'similarly to', 'inclined to', and 'such as':

   His typewriter is like a small airplane.
   It was like her not to come to the party.
   John always acts like a clown.
   It looks like rain today.
   a subject like physics

5. as an adverb with various meanings, including 'nearly' and 'rather':

   The actual interest is more like two percent.
   She sauntered over nonchalant like.

6. as a conjunction, usually meaning 'as' or 'as if':

- 37 -

She holds her pencil like most people hold
a toothbrush.
He looked like he wanted a warm place to stay.

Examining the LAB and RTS materials, many instances of _like_ were found that could not be adequately character-ized in any of the above six ways.[1] One frequent use of the form was preceding numerical expressions:

(1)   like one more week
(2)   like five till eight
(3)   like twenty dollars
(4)   like- thirteen bucks
(5)   like thirty-eight indictments
(6)   like eighty million buildings
(7)   like four floors
(8)   like two parties
(9)   like three years
(10)   like eleven guys
(11)   like two- two blocks down
(12)   like three blocks
(13)   like five o'clock Thursday
(14)   like - one lane
(15)   like Seventeenth and Summit
(16)   like ninety, y'know
(17)   like ten years ago
(18)   like from twenty to thirty
(19)   like at six o'clock
(20)   like three weeks
(21)   like two years
(22)   like just one finger
(23)   like twelve years
(24)   like on the twenty-sixth
(25)   like two weeks before

But in other cases _like_ precedes non-numerical expressions:

(26)   like every other night
(27)   like uh quite a few songs
(28)   like - lots of singers
(29)   like every night
(30)   like every other weekend
(31)   like chilly enough to where they could possibly
       have a coat on
(32)   like tangible. They're _there_. I can hear (th)em.

and can be used in cases where what the speaker is saying is obviously imprecise:

(33) He's like maybe ... what ten or something?
Twelve? I don't know. (Chafe 1980:302)
(34) like it's right behind (us) in a way

These and other nonstandard uses of _like_ are often considered symptomatic of careless or meaningless speech, and
those who use _like_ in these ways have been criticized
for doing so by purists such as Newman (1974:15), who,
interestingly, chooses a numerical expression to exemplify
the abuse: _like six feet tall_ (cf. Major 1970:77: _like
two years_). But if nonstandard _like_ is only a meaningless
interjection (see White 1955:303; cf. Wentworth and Flexner
1975:319, Major 1970, Landy 1971, Wood and Hill 1979,
and even Wright 1857), why is it so common before numerical
expressions?

This use of _like_ is reminiscent of, though not equivalent to, its use as an adverb meaning 'nearly' (use #5
above), but _like_ in (1)-(34) does not carry the implication
'less than' conveyed by that definition; in fact, the
meaning 'nearly' seems more properly attributed not to
like itself but to the entire construction _more like_
+ (NP).

Note that, despite the frequent claims to the contrary, there is a specifiable semantic difference between
descriptions preceded by _like_ and identical descriptions
without _like_. For example, if someone applying for a
driver's license were asked by a clerk in a department
of motor vehicles, "How tall are you?", a reply of "I'm
like six feet tall" would probably lead the clerk to ask
for a more exact response. Apparently, then, _like_, at
least in this use, is not entirely without function.
While _six feet tall_ can be standardly used for heights
between roughly 5'11" and 6'1", in a situation where precision is called for, _six feet tall_ can serve as a relatively exact response, but _like six feet tall_ cannot.

For most of examples (1)-(34) it is reasonable to claim that _like_ is an adverb meaning 'approximately'. _Approximately_ or _about_ or _around_ can be substituted for _like_ in most of these cases without noticeably altering their meaning or acceptability. But the substitution of _approximately_ in other cases is not a happy one, especially when the examples are examined in their surrounding context.

For example, consider (7) in more detail:

(7')   SUE: You know that um - they've been living
              in this big three-story house with base-
              ments- like foor floors y(ou) know- gigantic
              house on Summit ...   (LAB-B,22)

It seems fairly clear here that the speaker is not saying simply that the house in question has, say, somewhere between three and five floors, which is normally what would be conveyed by the expressions _about four floors_ and _approximately four floors_. Rather, she says explcitly that the house has exactly three stories. We know from context, on the other hand, that she is concerned with the largeness of this house, referring to it as _big_ and _gigantic_. To further convey a sense of its largeness, it would be advantageous to include the basements in the description of the house. However, to simply say that the house has four floors would be an unusual use of _floors_, since basements are conventionally excluded when counting the number of floors. It appears that _like_ is used by SUE to indicate that she is using _four floors_ with a special meaning. If so, one could offer as a synonym for _like_ in (7') 'as it were' or 'so to speak'.

Consider another example:

(27') H: Is that (i.e. music) a secret ambition?
       C: Uh: yes. A matter of fact - right now

>   we've written like uh quite a few songs
>   y(ou) know.   (RTS,13)

Substitution of _about_ or _approximately_ before _quite a few_ would be odd in (27') because the quantification _quite a few_ expresses that the speaker finds the number of songs notably large, while _approximately_ allows as possibilities that the quantity was either more or less than quite a few. _Approximately quite a few_ is thus internally contradictory, roughly parallel to saying, "This lamp cost around twenty-six dollars and eleven cents". But the contradictoriness disappears if the use of _like_ here is assumed to be similar to its use in (7'), that is, if it is considered to express the possibility that _quite a few_ may be an imprecise or inappropriate rendering of what the speaker has in mind. A similar argument can be constructed for (28): _like - lots of singers_.

Substitution of _approximately_ or _about_ is also quite odd in (22'):

> (22')   EVA: My dog a lotta times when we're playin(g)
>   (a)n(d) stuff y(ou) know (m- b- h-) my
>   hand'll get into (h)is mouth or: like
>   just one finger or sump'm like that ...
>   (LAB-B)

Just as in the case of _like quite a few_ and _like - lots of singers_, _like just one_ is internally contradictory if _like_ has the meaning 'approximately', since _just_ conveys the opposite. But there is again no contradiction if _like_ indicates simply that the speaker's words are an inexact portrayal of what the speaker has in mind, rather than conveying that one is appoximately the number of fingers involved.

A further indication that _like_ is not equivalent to _approximately_ or _about_ is that these other items can co-occur without any particular redundancy resulting:

> (35)   And that (.2) the little boy is like approx-
>   about ten years old (Chafe 1980:305)

Like in all of the above cases can be described as
indicating a possible discrepancy between what the speaker
is about to say and what the speaker feels ideally might
or should be said. _Like_ in this use can be seen as a
device available to speakers to provide for a loose fit
between their chosen words and the conceptual material
their words are meant to reflect. _Like_ with this use
is thus similar to the evincive items discussed in Chapter
2 in that it specifies a general connection between talk
and unexpressed thought. More specifically, the hypothesis
to be examined below is that _like_ is used to express _a_
possible unspecified minor nonequivalence of what is said
and what is meant. In cases where _like_ precedes an exact
numerical expression, it seems therefore to constitute a
kind of 'hedge'[2], attenuating the overexactness of the
speaker's chosen formulation; in the cases where _like_
precedes obviously inexact formulations, it indicates
that the speaker is aware that what follows is an imprecise
rendering of what s/he has in mind.

The remainder of this chapter will explore how far
one can get in understanding the conversational functions
of _like_ by applying this evincive treatment to the various
nonstandard instances of _like_ in the present data. It
should be noted that several of the standard uses of _like_
mentioned at the beginning of this chapter share with
evincive _like_ the notion of approximation, so that evincive
like can be viewed as related to the standard uses of
the form.

The double duty of _like_ as both a nonevincive comparative item and an evincive is not unusual. In the next
section parallels in several other languages are discussed.
But consider here as an initial example the form _nymiš_
in the West Central dialect of Sierra Miwok (Freeland
and Broadbent 1960:61; cf. Freeland 1951:169) which means
'like' but is also used to mean 'as it were':

(36) mu-uj-nymiš 'in the trail, as it were'

Forms usually meaning 'like' but also translatable as 'about' are also found. In the Sino-Tibetan language Lahu (Matisoff 1973:135), the form ghe can mean 'about', as in

(37) ŋǎ ɠǎ ghe
five (people counter) like
'about five people'

although it is also used to mean 'like', as in

(38) yǎ-ɛ ghe te ve
small child like do INDIC.
'He acts like a child'

Likewise, in Raluana, spoken in New Britain (Lanyon-Orgill 1960:134), the form dǎ generally has the meaning 'like', as in

(39) i mal dǎ rǎ parau
he dresses like (a) white man

but note its use in the following example:

(40) dǎ ravinun
like ten
'about ten'

3.2 Like Introducing Direct Discourse

A second use of nonstandard like in the present data is to introduce a direct quotation:

(41) Both sides o(f) the street can hear her yellin(g) at us and she's like "Come in here (a)n(d) have a beer" y(ou) know? [LAB-A,6]

(42) so I go "Um (:stylized) - Mom (a)n(d) Dad got me pants just about like that and I've worn those already", hint hint, y(ou) know. I was like "Come on, Dummy" [LAB-A,18]

(43) he goes "I'm sorry but you've only got seventeen dollars in here" - and I'm like "WHAT!!! I THOUGHT I HAD SIXTY DOLLARS IN THERE!!!" [Laughs] [LAB-A,21]

(44) It's not that she minds it so much. She's like "Well why ( ) waste all that gas. You know you

- 44 -

can find a ride home with somebody else". (LAB-A, 37)

(45) he kep- talkin(g) about how "Oh we're livin(g) together next year=it'll be so much easier for us cuz nobody else'll be around" and I'm just like "Buzz, aw" y(ou) know. (LAB-A,50)

(46) I came back an(d) called the police an(d) they told me - that it was there an(d) it was gonna be thirty-six bucks to get it out - an(d) I was just like "Oh my Go::d" (LAB-A,61)

(47) An(d) then on the way home it started snowin(g). It was terrible on the way home - I was drivin(g) twenty-five miles an hour - an(d) I was just like (i::::)" And then ... (LAB-A,63)

This use of <u>like</u> appears not to have been described previously in the literature[3]; I do not know its distribution, but it is at least very common among younger speakers in Central Ohio, where the present data were gathered.[4] The construction apparently cannot precede indirect discourse:

(48) ?He was like that he wanted to leave early.

and, if so, the quotative use of <u>like</u> is similar to narrative <u>go</u> 'say' (see 2.4) in being potentially useful as an enquoting device.

But examples (41)-(47) are not ordinary quotations. Speakers who use this construction claim that it prefaces not direct retrospective reports of speech, but internal speaker reactions--what the speaker had in mind to say but did not, or how the speaker felt at the time. One user of the construction suggested that it reports the speaker's "attitude". Thus what <u>like</u> in its quotative use introduces is a direct discourse rendering of what someone was thinking. It is as if the speaker were saying, "What I am about to report is <u>like</u> what I or someone else had in mind". Even when the item is used in the past tense:

(49) I was like "Oh my Go::d"

(50) I was like, "Come on, Dummy!"

like mediates between some former attitude the speaker now recalls and some immediately following suggestive or inexact formulation of this in the form of an 'internal' quotation.

Some recent comparative work offers an interesting line of support for this analysis of the origin of _like_ preceding direct discourse in English. Joseph (1981) argues that Hittite _(i)-wa(r)_, a particle introducing direct discourse, is related to Sanskrit _iva_ 'like, as', citing a claim by MacDonnell that _iva_, in addition to meaning 'like' or 'as' in similes, was used to modify "a statement not intended to be understood in its strict sense" (MacDonnell 1971:219-20). Joseph suggests that the similarity of _(i)-wa(r)_ and _iva_ lies in the fact that both particles "inject into the discourse elements of what the speaker has in mind". This consideration of the uses of _(i)wa(r)_ and _iva_ therefore provides a striking parallel to the incipient use of _like_ in English to intro- duce internal quotations. All it would take for the En- glish quotative use of _like_ to become altogether congruent to the quotative use of _(i)wa(r)_ would be for an extension to occur from internal to ordinary quotation. In either case, though, these particles introduce direct discourse.

Joseph also adduces in support of his claim about _(i)wa(r)_ a similar particle meaning 'like' but with a quotative use in Tok Pisin (Woolford 1979:117):

(51)   Elizabeth i tok _olsem_, "Yumi mas kisim ol samting
       pastaim."
       'Elizabeth spoke thus, "We must get things
       first"'.

Olsem usually has the meaning 'like', as in

(52)   Em i kamap yangpela boi _olsem_ James.
       'He grew up (to be) a young boy _like_ James.'

And Joseph mentions a similar particle, _(na)be_, also discussed by Woolford (ibid. 118), in Buang, and the San-

skrit particle _iti_ which is used both as a quotative particle and in constructions like the following:

    (53)   Tvam ambaya   putra _iti_ pratigrhitah
            you   mother+INST son   like be-received
            'You have been received by my mother _like_ a son.'

To these examples may be added the Lahu form _qhe_, already
mentioned, which Matisoff (1973:134) refers to as "the
most general and versatile of all Lahu words of comparison
... usually translatable as 'like', 'as', or 'thus'",
as in (38).[5] _qhe_ is used to close quotations:

    (54)   "te mâ phè?" _qhe_ qô? pî   ve   yo
            do not able like say BENEF INDIC DECL
            '"Cannot do it", thus he said'

qhe may represent a close parallel to English quotative
like'; that is, it may be restricted to use with internal
quotations. Matisoff (ibid. 468) mentions that of the
two quotative particles _tè_ and _qhe_, the former is most
likely to appear with longer and more complicated quotations. It is precisely quotations of length and complexity
that are most unlikely to be internal. Examples of English
quotative _like_ seem all to involve simple, brief broad-
stroke sketches of a speaker's attitude.

    Because of the similarities in Tok Pisin, Buang,
Sanskrit, and Lahu, it appears that the parallel between
Hittite _(i)wa(r)_ and quotative _like_ is not accidental
but reflects a functional correspondence (cf. Joseph and
Schourup 1982). In all five languages an item meaning
'like' does double duty as a quotative particle.

    The extension of quotative _like_ in English from inter-
nal quotations to quotations in general would not represent
a conventionalization of the item at the loss of its proposed use (i.e. to indicate a possible minor nonequivalence
of what is said and what is meant). As argued in Chapter
2, speakers are aware of the inexact nature of retrospec-

tive quotations; in view of their inexactness, it is perfectly appropriate to indicate that what the speaker reports as having occurred is only _like_ what may have actually been said. Thus, whether or not the Hittite, Sanskrit, Tok Pisin and Buang cases began as restricted to internal quotation, these languages share with English the property of indicating the approximative nature of a direct discourse report by means of a form meaning 'like'.

3.3 _Like_ After Questions

In the following examples _like_ occurs following a question:

    (55) (Tape begins; conversation already in progress)
          SUE: Wesley Point.
          EVA: Last bonus weekend like?
          SUE: No it was um - What comes up? Labor Day?
                Weekend? (LAB-B,27)
    (56) SUE: An(d) h(h)e g(h)ot th(h)e b(h)ir(h)d.
          EVA: In (h)is mouth like?
          SUE: In (h)is mouth. But he ditn('t) (h)ave
                a _chance_ to bite _down_ on (h)im. (LAB-B,21)
    (57) SUE: What radio station do you listen to?
          EVA: When I'm down here I listen to Dayton/When
                I'm at home I listen to Akron.
          SUE: ( ) Yeah but which one like.
          EVA: W. Oh! W.N.Q.X.'... (LAB-B,27)

These are the only examples in the present data in which _like_ is linked to a preceding sentence. In all three instances the speaker is soliciting clarification of something said by the speaker just previous to her. In the first two examples the speaker asks whether the formulation in the question is discrepant with respect to what the previous speaker intends. These examples are therefore also characterizable by the proposed evincive reading, the only difference being that, since the utterance to which _like_ is attached is a question, it is understood with reference to what the other speaker has in mind (note, though, that a possible discrepancy is implied between the <u>questioner's</u> proposed formulation and what the <u>questioner</u> feels the previous speaker meant). The difference between <u>like</u> in statements and questions reflects a general difference between questions and statements, not a difference between two uses of <u>like</u>. The third example differs from the other two in that <u>like</u> was spoken with low stress and pitch. The speaker seems to express a possible discrepancy between the question she is asking and what she thinks it would have been ideally appropriate to ask.

The <u>Oxford English Dictionary</u> lists as dialectal and vulgar the parenthetical use of <u>like</u> after a statement, citing 19th century examples, including <u>in an ordinary way like</u> and <u>If your honour were amongst us, there might be more discipline like</u>, attributing to these instances a meaning essentially equivalent to the general one proposed above for evincive <u>like</u>: "as it were; so to speak". Partridge (1970:482) specifies the meaning of <u>like</u> in this position as "somewhat, not altogether: as it were, in a way; in short, expressive of vagueness or after-thoughted modification". Although the post-sentential 'tag' uses of <u>like</u> cited in these two sources follow declaratives, the approximative reading seems equally applicable following questions, with the only difference being attendant on differences between questions and statements. In view of the small number of examples in the present sample, it may be accidental that only interrogative instances occur.

3.4 The 'For Example' Use

Many instances of <u>like</u> appear to have the meaning 'for example', among them the following[6]:

   (58)   C: The trucks are speeding on the side streets
                y(ou) know that are one-way (a)n(d) then

there's a wide at the end of it - y(ou) know
that there go out like on - oh Broadway for
instance or Fifth, or something like that
[RTS,10]

(59) J: Yeah. Because see l- a lotta people like
in business or other - uh things like that,
they get internships y(ou) know for the sum-
mers. [LAB-B,3]

(60) C: Y(ou) know um - besides taking care of groups
of people or - um y(ou) know uh I'm speaking
in like a secretarial situation - where you're
working for - y(ou) know you're you're h-
having to - set up your time ... [RTS-1]

(61) C: People would be - would come from all areas
- of the um of the States - an(d) uh and
uh so I would work in (th)e Graceland Club
an(d) and some people would like uh - to
hear like uh bluegrass music - so we would
do a - a little bit of like uh uh uh uh l-
little bluegrass-flavored music [RTS,14]

(62) SUE: I mean you don't have to get something
really expensive. Just go to um - like
Petrie's- Or that's/ not what that's
called.

EVA: Marianne's. [LAB-A,12]

(63) C: ...I'm just wondering like - if somebody
can get this close to the Pope who really
wants to kill (h)im what's gonna stop him
from say- say like throwing a knife at (h)im
or something and hitting him [RTS-1X,2]

In some of these examples the 'for example' reading is
strongly reinforced by context. In (58) <u>for instance</u>
appears, as does <u>oh</u>$_2$ (see 2.2); in (59) that <u>in business</u>
is to be understood as an example is provided for by the
continuation <u>or other - uh things like that</u>; in (63) this
is indicated by <u>or something</u>, and by use of the interjection <u>say</u> (see James 1974 on <u>say</u>). However, even if these
guiding contextual elements are eliminated, the 'for example' reading can persist:

(64) These trucks ... go out like on Broadway
(65) a lot of people like in business
(66) what's gonna stop him from like throwing a knife
at (h)im ...

Can the 'for example' reading be regarded as a contextual interpretation of the usual evincive 'discrepancy' use? Since, for instance, on Broadway is not plausibly discrepant in being an imprecise representation with respect to what the speaker has in mind, the only remaining plausible discrepancy is that on Broadway is an accurate but selective representation, which is what the 'for example' reading suggests.

Since like in the treatment proposed here indicates some minor discrepancy between what is said and what is meant (roughly, 'What I say is like what I mean'), the 'for example' reading should be possible in any case where selectivity of report is conceivably the nature of the discrepancy; in certain contexts (e.g. (58)), this possibility looms larger than in others (e.g. (65)), and in some cases the 'for example' reading is clearly absurd:

    (67)   When he unbuttoned his pants they like fell
             to the ground.

It is difficult to adduce tests that will tell us whether the 'for example' reading is a distinct lexical meaning of like. The item does not lend itself to the usual ambiguity tests (a number of these are discussed in Zwicky and Sadock 1973). The position taken very tentatively here is that the 'for example' use of like involves simply the interpretation of evincive like in contexts where a reasonable kind of discrepancy that could be indicated between what is said and what the speaker has in mind is one of selective mention.

The 'for example' use is especially applicable in initial position, as illustrated in these examples:

(68) C: ...but just walkin(g) through the middle
        of a crowd y(ou) know. Now like at the air-
        port - uh - P.R., I don't think there's any
        way anybody could've attempted to knock off
        the Pope. (RTS,35)
(69) [Caller has been attempting to show that Michigan
     State fans are poor sports]
     C: I don't know Like just - Like when the Cleve-
        land State plays Michigan State - I mean
        right afterwards- there's - it sometimes
        it seems like it's worse - even when they
        win - y(ou) know. Like I heard that some
        o(f) the store - y(ou) know people that sold
        popcorn (a)n(d) stuff they're not gonna sell
        anythin(g) that's in a bottle [i.e., so the
        fans can't throw the bottles on the playing
        field]. (RTS3,4)
(70) [Caller is attempting to show that Michigan
     drivers are worse than Ohio drivers]
     C: I'm just sayin(g) - a few people - can really
        do some uh mean things on the highway -
        traffic hazards y(ou) know. - Like - um
        I was on the freeway the other day with uh: on
        a - halfway trip comin(g) home to Ann Arbor
        - some car cuts over on me - never even
        looked. (RTS1,4)
(71) [Caller is attempting to show that assassinations
     are very easy to carry out]
     C: If some_body_ really y(ou) know knew about
        that [i.e. doing papal blessings by television
        instead of in person] and uh y(ou) know sort
        o(f) like OK like they go in an(d) - strap
        y(ou) know uh on a - a light coat y(ou) know
        where it'd be like chilly enough to where
        they could possibly have a coat on - and
        put on a - little bit o(f) plastic explosive
        around (h)im - sayin(g) "OK y(ou) know "I'm
        gonna be gone." (RTS20,28)
(72) C: uh:b - you know I - uh - I think they could
        build a like a: - a plastic uh - walkway
        - for the Pope. Like when he was walkin(g)
        through that - uh that hotel last Thursday
        - to (h)is car they could've wrapped a bullet-
        proof - plastic ... shield - o(f) some sort
        - He'd still be out in public. (RTS34a,32)
(73) C: SUE: Uh Fred's - Fred is my supplier o(f)
        cigarettes, man. (H)e came up brings me
        a carton, I go home he'll buy me at least
        two or three packs a week. I mean, like

> Saturday night he'll - buy me three packs
> o(f) cigarettes ... then - the next - I see
> (h)im almost every weekend ... [LAB-A,28]

The claim that these are all cases of sentence-initial
like admittedly involves some interpretation, but they
seem at least not to be clause internal. For the only
other initial-seeming *like* in the data, the 'for example'
reading is at least plausible (i.e. the reading of (74)
on which 'she' only sometimes works six days before getting
a two-day break):

> (74) I told her anytime she could come down y(ou)
>   know? But - I have to - the hours she works
>   - She got two days off in a row. Like she would
>   work six days an(d) then ... [LAB-B,28]

Schiffrin (1981a:11) has claimed that *like* is a 'non-
causal marker of evidence'. This characterization only
seems well suited to initial *like*, which has a 'for example'
reading. Schiffrin's characterization does not seem substantially different from the present one: an example
is, after all, a bit of non-causal evidence.

Initial *like* appears to have become routinized with a
selective mention use; the more general discrepancy reading
has been taken over by the related item 'It's like', which
is found only in initial position (cf. 3.6).

3.5 *Like* as an Interjection

The most often cited 'empty' slang use of *like* is
utterance initial:

> (75) Like, we was up in this freak's pad, man, and
>   she came off real lame. (White 1955:303)
> (76) Like do you understand? (Landy 1971:120)
> (77) Like, man, I was out in Wyoming ... (Major 1970)

(The controversy over this use of *like* should not be con-
fused with the unworthy debate, smouldering through most
of this century, over whether or not it is proper to use

like as a conjunction. See Whitman 1974; Krapp 1925:239-40; Literary Digest 1937; Bryant 1962; Follett 1966; Copperud 1980.)

Aside from the 'for example' instances in (68)-(74) there are in the present data a number of other instances of *like* that are clause-initial but follow some prefatory material:

(78)   but I found like that helped me a lot
(79)   so like basically people can differentiate
(80)   I'm just wondering like - if somebody can
(81)   (be)cause like some countries - y(ou) know
(82)   and y(ou) know like say right now he
(83)   because like y(ou) know he has a bulletproof
       vest
(84)   I mean like Saturday night he'll
(85)   but like - it's right behind us
(86)   And like before I met Fred (h)e was always
(87)   and well like Robbie's goin(g)
(88)   (be)cause like - he'll just he'll fly in your
(89)   y(ou) know an(d) - like he buzzed her
(90)   I mean- and you know like - most peo- an(d)
(91)   So like I- I- I- could
(92)   W(e)ll like um - with my brother-in-law
(93)   Well like I p- y(ou) know play tennis
(94)   So like if you play song-one song-two song-three

In some of these cases the 'for example' reading is com-pletely inappropriate (in (89), for instance, *like* precedes a problematical descriptive term; 'buzzing' is not one of many things that could have been mentioned, but one way of designating what the speaker's sister's dog did to a parakeet on a particular occasion). It is over cases like these that the accusation of meaninglessness waits most menacingly and in which it is most tempting to label *like* 'hesitative' or 'procrastinative' (as does Urdang 1979:78; cf. Landy 1971:120; Major 1970:77; Woolford 1979: 123[7]).

The fact that so many of these *like*'s occur after some prefatory material suggests that *like* is a pausal interjection. In a study of hesitations in spontaneous conversation Boomer, expecting to find hesitations more

numerous at the beginnings of phonemic clauses, found
instead that "the greatest frequency of hesitations is
not at the outset but at position 2, after the first word
of the clause" (Boomer 1965:151). The probable reason
for this is that a speaker may wish to begin a constituent
before having fully planned it, because beginning at all
preserves the turn by signaling the speaker's intention
to continue, while not beginning risks loss of the turn.
Similar reasoning can be applied to many of the post-prefa-
tory uses of like in (78)-(94). It is particularly notable
that in so many cases like occurs following a conjunction,
the use of which clearly indicates intended continuation.

If like can serve as a pausal interjection, this
would also explain why it is frequently followed by filled
and unfilled pauses. There are in the data 25 instances
of like immediately followed by filled and/or unfilled
pause, as in:

(95)   They may not be nice - y(ou) know like - um so
       nice. But they have nice dresses. [LAB-A,12]

In only seven cases is like preceded by a pause. There
are, moreover, several instances of like preceding a re-
start (a point at which the present speaker stops an item
under construction and recommences):

(96)   This like- This movie takes place in 1968
(97)   What we do is like- We did a uh

Three distributional facts point to the usefulness of
like in positions of pausal interjection: its occurrence
a) preclausally but after prefatory material; b) before
filled and unfilled pauses; and c) before restarts. Moreover, like is odd in positions in which pausal interjections are in general odd (see James 1974:150-1); that
is, like is odd in positions in which a pause to consider
how to continue would be unmotivated:

- 55 -

(98) *Not, like, only did John go, but he took all his stuff with him.
(99) *I did, like, not!
(100) *Get out of here, and if you don't obey, like, me, I'll sock you.
(101) *It's Julie's birthday today. We're giving, like, her a surprise party.
(102) *Jack flies planes carefully, but I do, like, so with reckless abandon.

Interjectional use of _like_ seems to be a conventional-ized way in which many speakers handle the recurrent situa-tion in which they intend to continue an utterance but find it difficult to formulate the continuation. Notice that _like_, at least as used currently[8], sounds peculiar before material that is easily formulable:

(103) Q: Were you born in Austria?
A: Like no.

The evincive reading of _like_ is not strongly present in many of examples (78)-(94), but this reading is not entire-ly irrelevant either. Coulmas (1981:2) writes of "the delicate double analyzability of many routine formulae". In the case of the routine use of _like_ as a pausal inter-jection, the double analyzability is of an interesting kind that can shed light on the reason for the routiniza-tion of the item. Notice that the evincive reading of _like_ is very generally applicable and appropriate in conversation because it is not limited to use in a highly specific set of contexts. _Like_ with this reading finds itself potentially at home in almost any utterance. The interjectional use of _like_ may have acheived such great popularity with some speakers precisely because of this. Such speakers may use for hesitation forms the basic con-tribution of which will not importantly alter what they are saying, but nevertheless have the virtue of being words, so that by using them they can still be heard as 'saying something' even if a proper formulation of their

- 56 -

thoughts for the moment eludes them (cf. Jefferson 1973:
69 on the notion of 'utterance lengthener').

The position taken here is that interjectional _like_
makes a substantive contribution to the utterances in
which it occurs: _like_ can be used as a routine hesitation
formula but can serve this purpose because its core evincive use is both widely applicable and relatively innocuous
to the proceedings. A speaker saying _like_ during a pause
to formulate a continuation subtly suggests a reason for
the pause: the material about to follow[9] is difficult
to formulate appropriately or precisely. This is implied
by the proposed evincive reading of the item. Unlike
well and $\underline{oh}_1$ (Ch. 2) _like_ is not predominantly an initiator, because formulation difficulties can and frequently
do arise within an utterance or sentence. It is not
surprising that _like_ is found in many other positions
beyond the favored ones already mentioned.

(104)   He was just- like losing it (LAB-A,16)
        I was able to like a(d)just (RTS,12)
        he like magnified it (RTSa,4)
        he like scuffed up against ... (LAB-B,16)
        it w- like bled a little bit (LAB-B,16)
        We have like rabbits that hop (LAB-B,24)
        It has to do with like uh things (RTSa,9)
        He's wearing like an apron (Chafe 1980:301)
        I can hear like a buzzing (LAB-B,19)
        He was like shy (RTSa,3)
        get like really heavy or serious (RTSa,1)
        eating like Chinese food (RTSa,6)
        we had like wicker baskets (Chafe 1980:309)
        who'd actually been like--good samaritains (Chafe
           1980:317
        with like - store levis (LAB-A)
        We'd leave like early so I could ... (LAB-A,16)
        He was like very funny (RTSa,6)
        We're gonna be like basically uh (RTSa,8)
        You see him - like - at a- at a distance (Chafe
           1980:302)
        supposed to have like a Cambodian character
           (RTSa,4)
        playing like with - I don't remember (Chafe
           1980:309)

> There's like this situation   (RTSa,3)
> everything's like thrown off   (RTSa,8)

To say that the evincive use of _like_ can be latent--
accessible and relevant, but not prominent--amounts to pro-
posing that we must speak of degrees of meaningfulness,
literalness, or usefulness. If we consider the literal
meaning of lexical hesitation forms to have been completely
superseded by their routine function, we must account for
the unimaginability of, say, _rubber_ or _four_ as hesitation
forms.[10] (See also the discussion of this topic in 1.4.)

Twenty-two subject volunteers were queried to determine to what extent, if any, they were able to assign
a particular use or meaning to _like_ in some of its nonstandard positions of occurrence. It was reasoned that even if
the evincive reading is latent rather than nonexistent,
it should be accessible to some extent when subjects have
a chance to scrutinize an utterance containing _like_.
Students in an introductory linguistics course were asked
to consider the word _like_ in the following six conversation
excerpts, which were presented in written form:

(105)   She was very like open about her past.
(106)   There was like nothing in any of the cupboards.
(107)   So like after the game we went down to the Char
         Bar
(108)   Dorothy is like constantly asking for attention.
(109)   Oh fine. Except Ralph like kept kicking me
         under the table.
(110)   No matter what they say, I'll be like ... flat-
         tered.

Subjects were asked to write down the meaning, if any,
of _like_ in each of the example sentences. They were given
as much time as they needed.

Although the 'meanings' assigned to _like_ differed
from speaker to speaker and from example to example, virtually all were consistent with the evincive reading in
which _like_ indicates a possible minor nonequivalence

of what is said and what is meant. The responses, however, tended to be quite specific about the particular discrepancies involved. For example, subjects agreed that in (105) _like_ somehow suggested a special meaning for _open_, but disagreed about what that special meaning was. One speaker suggested 'indirectly open'; another, 'very open but very blunt'; another, 'open, as you may have known other people to be'; another, 'almost very open'. One speaker even suggested that openness was only one of the qualities involved (the 'for example reading'). In each case _like_ was understood as conveying a difference between the speaker's words and what the speaker had in mind.

Similar disagreements were found regarding the meaning of _like_ in (106). Subjects understood _like_ as conveying that _nothing_ was being used with a special sense. Some of the suggested meanings: 'nothing worth having', 'nothing of importance', 'nothing that had appeal or value to the speaker', 'nothing the person wanted', 'nothing of interest or usefulness', 'nothing that she likes', 'almost nothing', 'it just seemed like nothing', 'absolutely nothing'. What these responses have in common is, again, that they include an extra element of meaning beyond what _nothing_ ordinarily conveys. Two subjects thought that _like_ conveyed that the speaker was surprised or amazed at how empty the cupboards were.

Like in (107) was taken to qualify _after the game_. Some of the suggested meanings: 'not immediately after', 'a while after', 'soon after but not immediately', 'not immediately following'. Two subjects assigned the 'for example' reading.

Subjects disagreed about whether _like_ in (108) expressed qualifications about _constantly_ or emphasized it. One subject felt that _like_ conveyed that the speaker felt the questioning to be 'a burden'. Similar disagreements over the precise contribution of _like_ were found with regard to the extent of the kicking in (109); some subjects felt that _like_ emphasized the amount of kicking that occurred, while others felt that it was less than _kept kicking me_ seemed to indicate.

In a few cases subjects offered more general meanings, also consistent with the evincive reading:

(111) "Speaker is unsure of how to say what he means" (re:(110))
(112) "hesitant to say what you know" (re:(111))
(113) "gives the speaker room for qualification" (re:(111))
(114) "expects the listener to fill in" (re:(111))

In (110) _like_ is followed by periods, a conventional orthographic indication of pause. One subject noted that the speaker paused to think of the word _flattered_, but this subject nevertheless assigned _like_ a discrepancy reading: 'not _sure_ he'll be flattered'. Another subject suggested that _like_ "shows a comparison with a word not there, maybe a word similar to _flattered_'. Another suggested that _like...flattered_ means 'as if flattered'. Yet another suggested, 'She feels she is flattered but is not sure if that is the way she should take it'. Another: 'really wonders whether he'd be flattered or not'.

These results indicate that even if the basic use of _like_ is not consistently or clearly accessible to introspection, when a reading _is_ assigned in a situation of close attentiveness, the use attributed to the form is essentially the proposed one.

3.6 It's like

There are several instances of sentence-initial _it's like_ in the data, in which _it_ has no clear discourse or situational referent (no referent, that is, such as _hot car_ in _Carmelita has a hot car. It's like the one that Cecil bought._). Rather, _it's like_ appears to have the same evincive reading that _like_ has by itself. In the

following examples the pronoun _it_ can be taken to refer
to what the speaker has in mind to express:

(115) H: Does he thwart you at any time? Y(ou) know
           w- things that he says?
       C: Uh n::ot really. It's like uh:: uh::m uh
           in a playful - kind o(f) way I guess - y(ou)
           know (RTSa,1)
(116) H: It doesn't even get to the point where you
           kind o(f) do a double take? ...
           Uh y- Well - It's like w(e)ll sometimes
           that does happen. (RTSa,3)
(117) They tailor-made it uh - _for_ us - almost - y(ou)
       know. It's like they wrote it around us.
       (RTSa,3)
(118) I mean like uh:: - I I like to use all kin(d)
       o(f) pipes - Ex- Excuse the expression - y(ou)
       know like uh y(ou) know wha(t) I- It's like
       what is that thing called? A 'buyer'? (RTSa,5)
(119) An(d) it's like - y(ou) know it's (j)us(t)
       (n-) - ya can't pass anybody anyway. It's one
       o(f) them- It's like- the road I live on here
       in Ohio y(ou) know like - one lane or y(ou)
       know it's two-way (ya gotta) go off the side
       o(f) the road for anything to pass ... and it's
       like - It's just kind o(f) wild. (LAB-A,64)
(120) H: How does a guy from Cheyenne find relating
           to let's say a Barbara Streisand kind of
           an audience? Uh - an easy or a hard job.
       C: W- It's like when I went into the service
           - I went in the Marines - we were - (tells
           story) (RTS,13)
(121) H: Is that a secret ambition? (i.e. doing
           a musical routine)
       C: Uh: yes. - But it's like uh right now we've
           written like uh quite a few songs. (RTS,13)
(122) I met Charlie Goodrich and it's like I met him
       at Aspen ... (RTS,6)
(123) and uh y(ou) know it's like uh:m we did a thing
       on the Ed Sullivan Show. (RTSa)

     Two additional examples of _it's like_ appear in the
data, preceding internal quotation (cf. 3.2):

(124) It's like "Oh God. There's all these people
       walking by" hhh. (LAB-A,6)
(125) People wouldn't touch her for years because
       it's like "Oh she's a singer" y(ou) know. (RTSa)

Note that, just as _like_ does, _it's like_ frequently occurs before hesitations and other discontinuities. In all but two of examples (115)-(123) _it's like_ precedes a discontinuity of one kind or another. The only difference between _it's like_ and _like_ seems to be that _it's like_ is restricted to clause- (and usually sentence-) initial position (cf. 3.4).

3.7 Conclusion

In the preceding discussion it is argued that the current efflorescence of _like_ in conversation, at least among younger speakers, is not a symptom, as Newman would have it, of "the death of English", but the spread from its originally quite restricted range of occurrence of an item which in general indicates a possible loose fit between overt expression and intended meaning. With this use _like_ is particularly suited to conversation, where speakers (even, probably, Edwin Newman) frequently find themselves in the position of having to formulate what they have to say without time for the considered eloquence possible when they are, say, hunched over a manuscript. The exigencies of speech, and even sometimes of writing, often call for such eminently acceptable locutions as _so to speak_ and _as it were_, which, by rights, ought to be subject to as much censure as _like_ insofar as they too can indicate speakers' inability to formulate a strictly accurate or appropriate version of what they want to express. No doubt _like_ is the scapegoat of normativists because it is, at least in some positions of occurrence, a newcomer.

To claim that the 'aberrant' uses of _like_ are meaningless is simply wrong, though this charge may be leveled in a qualified way against the routine interjectional use of _like_ in which the evincive reading is less promi-

nent, though still appropriate. The charge of meaninglessness is, on the other hand, entirely unjustified in the
case of _like_ before, for example, numerical or obviously
inexact descriptions, _like_ in initial position where it
indicates partial report, and _like_ indicating an approximative internal quotation.

To the extent that evincive _like_ is a provision for
loose talk, it is understandable that its use has been
criticized. However, similar uses of _like_ have been observed for centuries in English[11]; and only a pedant would
insist that speakers ought to be always able to find the
perfect outward expression for their thoughts. In addition to _like_ and the more respectable expressions _as it_
were, _so to speak_, _more or less_, _in so many words_, _in_
a way, etc. (a list appears in G. Lakoff 1972), English
has at the moment _sort o(f)_, _kind o(f)_, _kind o(f) like_,
sort o(f) like, etc., all of which can under certain circumstances indicate a possible discrepancy between what
the speaker has in mind and what is overtly said (though,
there are often fine differences between particular
items).[12]

Nor can English be considered moribund for requiring
items that acknowledge flawed, or possibly flawed, expression. Speech is by nature a selective and often approx-
imate rendering of mental contents. Though there might
be a case made for some thoughts being perfectly expressed
by some wordings, it seems unlikely that such a perfect
connection exists as the rule. In any language one may
comment on this fact, but the situation arises so frequently in speech that languages also have more conventional
ways of dealing with it.[13]

Like thus joins the ranks of maligned conversational
items recently being resurrected under the comely title
'discourse particles'. Such items have a specifiable

use in conversation but do not lend themselves to static entries in dictionaries. Evincive _like_, as other evincives do, comes to life in the dynamics of ongoing talk with its temporal and turn-taking requirements, unexpected turns of topic, sleights, distractions, and on-the-spot negotiations. In this kind of behavior talk and thought frequently diverge, and it can be helpful to the ends of communication if speakers have a simple way of saying so, or of making it seem so.

Even as a pausal interjection _like_ has its peculiar virtues. Rather than just filling a hole in an utterance, it offers, at least insofar as its core use is attended to, a reason for the pause. By saying that what follows will be _like_ what should or could be said, the speaker suggests that some thought is difficult to formulate. By being explicated, the pause is detoxified, becoming polite and reasonable, an attempt at expression rather than a failure of communication.

CHAPTER FOUR
<u>WELL</u>

4.1 Introduction

In this chapter it will be argued that the discourse particle <u>well</u> is an evincive with a particular basic use and that this fact is crucial to understanding the various ways in which <u>well</u> is used in conversation. The discourse particle is to be distinguished from the adverb <u>well</u>, as in

(1) She swims well.

and the 'degree word' <u>well</u>, as in

(2) We were well into summer before the fog lifted.

The <u>well</u> discussed in this chapter is usually referred to as an interjection and has no obvious synchronic connection to the adverb or the degree word. The use of the discourse item is illustrated in (3) and (4):

(3) Well, I don't know.
(4) There were, well, four of them.

The discourse particle <u>well</u> has been the subject of several recent studies. Particular interest has been shown in the 'discourse function' of <u>well</u>, which has been examined by considering how the appearance of this item in an utterance (imagined or actual) alters the meaning, use, or appropriateness of the utterance. The usual result of these studies has been to isolate a number of putatively distinct uses of <u>well</u>, each representing the pairing of some identifiable discourse position and an aspect of the meaning or use of utterances containing <u>well</u> in that position. The great variety of such uses

- 64 -

has led, in addition, to general pronouncements about what these uses, or some subgrouping of them, have in common.

The principal aim of this chapter is not to dispute the accuracy or relevance of these previous studies, though some analyses will be questioned, but to propose a unified account of the many different discourse functions of well identified to date in the literature. As in the previous two chapters, this will involve having recourse to the notion 'evincive' (see, especially, Ch. 2), which, in the case of well, turns out to have considerable explanatory value. The issue to be addressed with regard to each of the discourse functions considered will be why well in particular is used to fulfill each specific discourse function. The authors of the functional studies of well to be referred to below have seemed content, with exceptions to be discussed, to treat well as if its function were entirely describable by characterizing the function of utterances containing it. It will be argued below that as an evincive well has in fact a single basic or core use and that in particular discourse contexts this core use can lead to a variety of possible interpretations based on the interaction of the basic contribution of the item with the contexts in which it occurs. The claim, then, is that once the core use of well has been correctly isolated, the 'functional polysemy' of the item is predictable and understandable.

If, as just claimed, well has a single isolable use, how has previous research overlooked it? The answer is probably that the basic contribution of well is not clearly accessible to introspection. For one thing, to adequately characterize the use of well, a speaker would have to correctly formulate its evincive status.

This is a lot to ask. Also, in reporting the meaning
of a sentence linguistically naive speakers do not carefully sort out pragmatic from strictly linguistic factors; even competent linguists find it hard to extricate
these two bedfellows. When speakers attempt to consult
their intuitions about the contribution of well, this
contribution is reported as an amalgam of the basic lexical contribution of the word and the implicatures and
contextual understandings relevant when that contribution
is used in situ (cf., in this regard, the meaning reports
in 3.5 above). A third possible reason contributing
to difficulty in reporting the contribution of well is
that interjections operate somewhere below the level
of full conscious awareness (unless they become so abun-
dant as to draw attention to themselves). Interjections
are not in general heard as crucial to the content of
an utterance and are, therefore, not faithfully reproduced in, for example, the retelling of a joke. Well
does not entirely resist introspection, of course, as
the studies discussed below attest. Differences between
utterances containing well and those, otherwise the same,
that do not, are noticeable, but they represent a combination of the basic contribution of well and contextual
interpretations of its use.

The proposal of this chapter is that the basic evincive use of well is to indicate that the present speaker
is now examining the contents of the private world.
The many distinct uses of well in discourse all share
this core use, though the net interpretation of an utterance containing well will only be explicable by answering
two questions: 1) Where in the sequential development
of a particular sentence, utterance, exchange, conversation, etc., does well occur? and 2) Why does the speaker
in that particular context and sequential position choose
to draw attention to his or her examination of the pri-

vate world? In the following sections each of the discourse functions that have been attributed to <u>well</u> is examined individually with a view to showing how each can be appropriately described by answering these two questions, provided that in each case <u>well</u> has the basic evincive use just proposed.

4.2   <u>Well</u> Before Exclamations

Svartvik (1980) takes <u>well</u> in examples like <u>Well I'm damned</u> (cf. American English <u>Well I'll be damned</u>) to be an expression of "exclamatory surprise, etc." (173) and considers this use of <u>well</u> distinct from its other uses. Notice, however, that the expression <u>I'm damned</u> alone conveys exclamatory surprise, so that there is really no clear case for <u>well</u> itself having this meaning. It can be suggested that <u>well</u> is common before items like <u>shit</u>, <u>gee whiz</u>, and <u>hell</u>, because such items are only appropriately uttered when the speaker has clear justification for resorting to emotionally charged language. Because <u>well</u> expresses that the speaker is engaged in private thinking, and does this just prior to the exclamatory utterance, <u>well</u> can be taken here to indicate that grounds for strong language exist. <u>Well</u> does not itself indicate what these grounds might be-- it indicates only that what the speaker says is immediately preceded by internal consultation.

The interpretation of <u>well</u> in this case can be broken down further in a way that will also be useful to apply to other functions of <u>well</u>:

BASIC INTERPRETATION PATTERN FOR 'WELL'
1.   <u>Well</u> indicates speaker's current consultation of the private world (the core use);
2.   since this inward consultation is evinced by a lexical item, it is inferably related in some way to the linguistic proceedings;

3. since the marker of internal consultation is placed before and after sequentially placed contributions of talk, _well_ is inferably relevant _in sequence_;
4. an addressee may attempt to discern a reason why the speaker has used a marker of internal consultation at a given sequential position in a conversation and, in assuming that the speaker is being cooperative, may try to deduce the reason for the consultation being evinced by use of _well_ rather than brought up explicitly in the shared world; and the speaker using _well_ may expect such inferences and deductions (or guesses) to occur and matter to the interaction.

In the particular case of _Well I'm damned_, _well_ is heard as relevant to the uttering of _I'm damned_. Since _I'm damned_ is an expression of strong emotion, _well_ is inferably used here in an attempt to justify the employment of this charged item in the shared world. The speaker appears to be saying, "I'm not simply losing control of myself here--there is a good reason, which I am now internally consulting, for my choice of this emotive expression." The specifics of the justification that _well_ evinces will in some cases be apparent to both speaker and interlocutors. For example, _Well I'm damned_ could be spoken after another's shocking announcement. But these details may also be something to which only the speaker is privy--for example, if _Well I'm damned_ were uttered when the speaker had just felt an ectopic heart beat or suddenly noticed a close visual resemblance between some other conversant and Marie Curie.

The Basic Interpretation Pattern given above will be alluded to repeatedly below in the discussion of other uses of _well_; it always applies in the same way, although the particulars in item 4 will differ from context to context. Note that no claim is being made that speakers sequentially apply these steps in real time; the intent is simply to enumerate the factors involved in a contextual interpretation of _well_.

4.3 <u>Well</u> Introducing Direct Discourse

Svartvik comments that <u>well</u> is used as a "signal
indicating the beginning of direct speech, parallel to
that of quotation marks in writing" (1980:175). It was
argued above in Chapter 2 that <u>well</u> in this position
has simply its basic evincive use. Strictly, it is correct in one way, and incorrect in another, to compare
the use of <u>well</u> to that of quotation marks--correct in
that <u>well</u> can perform the enquoting function (see 2.4),
but incorrect in that <u>well</u> is attributed to the quoted
speaker. Subjects presented with example sentences like
(5) overwhelmingly assign <u>well</u> to the quotation:

> (5) Roger said, "Well, think it over and let me
> know Tuesday."

Moreover, to claim that <u>well</u> is simply an enquoting mark
fails to explain why many other evincive interjections
are capable of serving the same function (see 2.2.1).

It was argued in Chapter 2 that <u>well</u> is in general
a construction on the part of the quoting speaker inserted by that speaker as backgrounding for the substantive part of the quotation (but intended and heard as
attributed to the quoted speaker). Evincive <u>well</u>, because it calls into play the Basic Interpretation Pattern
is useful to contextualize a quotation by providing a
background against which it can be appreciated. Via
the Pattern, <u>well</u> invokes a situation in which the quoted
speaker may be seen as having spoken out of some then-
current consideration and it thereby helps to situate
the quotation as an integral part of some nonpresent
situation.

Goldberg (1980:113) suggests a similar, but importantly different function of <u>well</u> in utterances like
(5). "Perhaps it is because the <u>well</u> ties the utterance-
unit back to the preceding utterance-unit that <u>well</u> often

prefaces reported speech. The quote is used to support or add colour to what has been related." First notice that, as Svartvik did, Goldberg disregards the fact that well is attributed to the quoted rather than the quoting speaker. If it links anything to something prior, therefore, it should be seen as linking the quoted utterance to something prior for the quoted speaker in the reported situation of utterance, not the contribution of the quoting speaker. If such well's were to be heard as a linking device for tying together utterances of the quoting speaker, we would expect well to occur somewhere before, not after, the verb of verbal communication, since occurring after that verb well is assigned to the quoted speaker (see 2.4).

Note also that Goldberg's comment concerns the utterance-unit containing well rather than well itself. The principal force of her work on well and other discourse particles has been to demonstrate the collocation of these items with particular types of conversational 'moves'[1] and the interpretation of particles as 'markers' of these move types. In the case of well introducing direct quotation, this leads away from the basic sense of well to an attempt to see well as a marker of a 'holding' or a 'progressive holding' move:

> An utterance-unit is ... a holding move if it is a backchannel or if its discourse referents are drawn from those in the utterance-unit(s) which immediately preceded it, that is, referents may be "subtracted" or dropped but new referents may not be added; (an utterance is) a progressive-holding move if it shares some of the same discourse referents as the prior utterance-unit but also adds additional referents not present in the prior utterance-unit. (Goldberg 1980:89)

The treatment of well as a marker of move type involves a difficult step of reasoning (which proves equally problematic for Goldberg's treatment of y'know discussed below in Ch. 6): use of the word 'marker' implies that the item in question cues move type rather than that it is simply a frequent concomitant of certain move types. Presumably something referred to as a 'marker' is used by speakers specifically to mark move type and is understood that way by others. The weaker position, though it is the strongest position supported by Goldberg's data, is that well (because, I would claim, of its basic evincive use) is more likely to occur with some move types than others. The stronger 'marking' position would seem to require for its support a demonstration that conversants can actually identify move types by referring to well exclusive of following material. It seems unlikely that this could ever be demonstrated, however, since well in fact occurs with various move types and could not, therefore, unambiguously indicate any particular one.[2]

In the present case, the applicability of move analysis to well beginning quotations is ill-founded so long as the analysis attempts to relate the quoted utterance to foregoing material contributed by the quoting speaker. Such well's are more appropriately viewed as backgrounders (Ch. 2) that contextualize the quotation with respect to the quoted speaker's situation of utterance. Such backgrounders are in fact heard as speech attributed to the quoted, not the quoting, speaker.

4.4 Topic Shifting

Svartvik (1980:174) cites an example (here rewritten in reader's notation) in which well closes previous discourse and focuses on following discourse, offering as synonyms for this use 'all right then', 'so', 'ok', 'consequently':

(6) A: but if they wanted people around to talk

> to - then I would be very happy to sat -
> (and) got a letter back saying we have
> arranged for you to stay - Well let's
> take the interview first.

This can again be regarded as simply the use of evincive well according to the Basic Interpretation Pattern. Without well the speaker would be seen as peremptorily changing topic without taking leave of the other participant to do so. This might lead to unwarranted implicatures (for example, that the speaker is concealing something or is disturbed by the direction the conversation is taking). By evincing covert consultation at the point just before an abrupt topic shift, the speaker can imply that the shift is a considered one and, by announcing that the consideration is occurring, invokes interlocutors to fill in some reasonable motive for the shift (for example, that it is time to get to the business at hand).

Consider the following fabricated example:

> (7) B: ((talks about his new swimming pool))
> A: Do you have the merger papers with you?
> B: Yes. So I thought, "Nine feet? Sure, that's deep enough."
> A: Well, can we get started on this now?
> B: Oh, sure. I'm sorry. The papers are right here.

Goldberg (1980) includes cases of this sort with instances of well prior to continuations following side sequences (see Jefferson 1972), well initiating a (pre-) closing section (see Schegloff and Sacks 1973), and well introducing the first topic of a conversation. She comments, "Well marked moves are essentially 'backward looking' with a forward looking disposition--that is, well marked moves tie the current utterance-unit back to the prior utterance-unit(s) while providing informa-

- 73 -

tion which progresses the conversation into its next phase" (105).

It was suggested earlier that the fact that <u>well</u> ties previous to following material follows simply from the fact that it occurs after preceding material and before following material (as do all other conversational items except the first and the last) and, given the cooperativeness of speakers, is taken as relevant to the developing conversational sequence in the sense that the speaker is presumed to be mindful of what has been said and prospctively attentive to what is to be said next. Even items like <u>actually</u>, which specify a break with preceding material (see Goldberg 1980) are 'backward looking' insofar as they establish a break between what follows and what precedes.

Topic shifts, preclosings, closings, and changes from introductory to topic talk are all straightforwardly what they are. The <u>well</u> often prefixed to these moves indicates that the speaker makes whatever the move is with prior consideration. To mark this consideration as occurring at just that point has the effect of smoothing the transition to the next phase, but <u>well</u> has this effect only by virtue of its basic use applied in the particular context in which it occurs; by drawing attention to the considered nature of the shift, the speaker indirectly provides that the shift is a motivated one and thereby forestalls any possible accusations of noncooperativeness, peremptoriness, or lack of attention to the developing sequence of talk.

4.5 <u>Well</u> Before Answers

Noting the occurrence of <u>well</u> in examples such as (8) and (9),

(8)   What time is it?
       Well, the sun just came up.
(9)   Did you kill your wife?
       Well, yes.

Lakoff (1973:458-459) proposes that _well_ preceding an answer expresses either some kind of insufficiency in the answer itself, or that the answerer considers the question to be in some respect insufficient or deficient. Hines' treatment (1977) differs from Lakoff's in treating _well_ as an acknowledgment that the addressee has heard the question and grants the previous speaker's right to ask it. In either view it is expected that _well_ will frequently occur before indirect answers, as in (8): these answers might otherwise be in danger of seeming unresponsive or uncooperative.

Hines claims that if _well_ precedes a direct answer, it expresses either that the speaker is unsure whether the answer is responsive to all that is meant by the question, or that the question is itself deficient in some way--for example, in that it asks for information the questioner may be presumed to have already (see Hines 1977:311).

In Hines' treatment _well_ does not itself indicate insufficiency but rather is used to implicate insufficiency. For example, occurring before a direct answer, as in (10),

(10)   Q: What time is it?
       A: Well, three o'clock.

well is, in this view, heard as basically acknowledging the questioner's right to ask the question. If the answerer acknowledges the speaker's right to ask the question where such an acknowledgment is not obviously called for, as in (10), the answerer thereby implicates that the right to ask the question was questionable.

The evincive treatment of _well_ offers a simple explanation for why _well_ is found so commonly before indirect answers and after questions the answerer finds problematical. Again, the Basic Interpretation Pattern can be called into use. The primary fact here is that the speaker chooses to express that inner consultation is occurring prior to answering. Hines' term 'acknowledgment' is functionally apt in cases like this, but the evincive treatment explains why _well_ is capable of performing this acknowledgment.

Since _well_ evinces current inner consultation and is placed between the two parts of a question/answer sequence, between the question that just occurred and the answer that is about to, _well_ is inferably related to the question and/or the answer. In any case the question is taken into consideration and thus, in effect, acknowledged.

The evincive treatment also provides a reason for the sense of 'insufficiency'. To evince internal consultation at a given point embodies a claim by the speaker that to announce such consultation there is relevant. Since the expected response to a nonrhetorical question is a prompt and direct answer, any failure of a direct answer to follow the question in timely fashion implies difficulty on the speaker's part in answering. Either the meaning, appropriateness, etc. of the question, or the answering process, may be the source of the difficulty. We may predict, as a third case not mentioned by Lakoff or Hines, sequences in which _both_ question and answer are deemably insufficient. (11) is a hypothetical example:

> (11) Q: When did it all begin?
> A: Well, if you mean the universe, I don't
> think it had to have a beginning, _per se_.

That _well_ after questions implicates an insufficiency
follows from the fact that it is issued between the question and the response or answer. Labov and Fanshel (1977:
189) note that _well_ has a "temporizing and delaying"
function. This follows from the evincive treatment:
the speaker has paused to consult his or her thoughts.
If so, the speaker must have been 'given pause' by something. This will be interpretable as indicating some
insufficiency in the question or the answer or both.

4.6 _Well_ Before Questions

Lakoff (1973) comments that _well_ used before questions, as in

(12) Well, who's going to take out the garbage?

expresses insufficiency felt by the user of _well_ to obtain in the utterance or action to which the question
is a response. Here again, an interpretation invited
by a particular discourse context has been mistaken for
a property of the word _well_ itself. (12) conveys the
speaker's impatience (due to an insufficiency in the
existing situation). But why would the speaker of (12)
want to indicate inner consultation? The garbage needs
to be taken out (if this is a bona fide indirect request)
and nobody is clearly intending to do it (another condition on sincere requests). _Well_ is used to indicate
that the speaker's indirect request is based on consideration of the existing situation, which itself involves
an insufficiency. _Well_ does not convey the insuffi-
ciency--the question following _well_ implies it.
Or consider (13):

(13) Well, why didn't Harvard trounce 'em?

This _well_ merely indicates that "Why didn't Harvard
trounce 'em?" is a considered question. It is certainly

true that there is something lacking in the situation to which the question is a response, but does _well_ convey this? The question itself does so. If a question was asked, it must be because not all of the information the speaker of the question needs is apparent or has been provided. The only difference in meaning attendant on the use of _well_ here is that by saying _well_ the speaker expresses inner consultation for one of various reasons none of which is explicitly announced by _well_ itself, but which may thereafter be hinted at, implied, explained, or left hanging by the speaker, and for the addressee's part, may be guessed at, inferred, or left unquestioned. Since a question follows this announced inner consultation, the consultation is heard as leading to the question. The speaker appears to be saying, "On the basis of consideration, I am led to ask this..." But this interpretation is grounded in pragmatics: to understand how _well_ is used here, one must ask why it is that a speaker might 'announce' inner consultation prior to asking a particular question.

4.7 _Well_ and Self-Repair

Svartvik (1980:75) and Goldberg (1980:229) cite work by DuBois in which he claims that _well_ is one type of 'editing marker', specifically, a 'claim editing' marker, in contrast to markers of 'reference editing' (e.g. _that is_), 'nuance editing' (e.g. _rather_), and 'mistake editing' (e.g. _I mean_). The repair following a _well_ of this kind "embodies a modification from the less accurate, more excessive, flamboyant or exaggerated to the more moderate and accurate" (Goldberg 1980:229). This observation appears to be essentially correct; it may be pointed out, though, that once again the usefulness of _well_ for a particular discourse function (here, claim editing) is only understandable when the basic evincive use of <u>well</u> is taken into account.

Well does not itself directly indicate correction of any kind. Note the discourse context in which these instances of <u>well</u> are found: after a repairable item and before a correction. The occurrence together of a repairable and a correction, itself indicates that correction is being undertaken and what kind of correction is being made. To understand the role <u>well</u> plays in self-repair, it is only necessary to examine the consequences of inserting a marker of inner consultation between the two 'halves' of certain repair sequences. The other marker types mentioned by DuBois all serve their function by virtue of an element of meaning they bear. This is obvious from comparing the ascribed correction functions and the literal meanings of <u>I mean</u>, <u>that is</u>, and <u>rather</u>. As an evincive, <u>well</u> indicates looking inward at present mental contents. The repair cases in which inner consultations are most likely to be of use are those in which the speaker wishes to reconsider something s/he has just said and restate it more in accordance with those mental contents. This is all that <u>well</u> does at repair sites. The notion that the correction involved is more accurate, less excessive, etc. than the original is not a fact about <u>well</u>, or even about 'claim editing'; it is a fact about correction itself. Virtually all correction and editing involves improvements in the direction of more accuracy. To say that <u>well</u> marked repairs have this function is therefore not very illuminating.

Items like <u>I mean</u>, <u>that is</u>, and <u>rather</u> can help clarify the nature of a particular correction where this might be in doubt, but <u>well</u> indicates only that the speaker is reconsidering. The oddness of a correction like

(14)

(14)   ?I have a dog, well, a cat named Flora.

is due to the appearance it gives that the speaker is
reconsidering the zootaxy of his or her pet. Such semantic substitution errors arise when the speaker slips
and selects the wrong form from the mental lexicon.
Because the speaker of an error like that in (14) does
not mean cat as an inaccurate approximation of dog, no
reconsideration is necessary--only substitution of the
correct form. The item I mean is acceptable in semantic
substitution errors

(15)   I have a dog, I mean cat, named Flora.

precisely because it specifically clarifies (with its
literal reading) that the repairable is an incorrect
(not simply inaccurate) representation of what the speaker has in mind to say.

Not all self-repair involves correction. Well,
as noted by James (see 2.3 above), can occur at sentence-
internal points of pause:

(4)   There were, well, four of them.

Since the sentence is incomplete at the point where well
is issued, the inferable reason for the pause is that
the speaker has paused to consider how to continue the
sentence.

Although James in general defers to Lakoff (1973)
for discussion of the meaning of well, she does make
several comments regarding the sentence-internal use
of the item. (James' discussion of well is in fact limited to these sentence-internal uses, and she even claims
(1974:9) that well is primarily sentence-internal, although this could not be farther from the truth (see
Ch. 2).) One use of well mentioned by James is to indicate that "the speaker can be stopping to think of the
best way of saying what he has to say" (1974:17).   In

this use <u>well</u> is only acceptable "when the speaker could have said something other than what he does say; when there is thus a reason for him to stop and think". Interjectional <u>well</u> thus "implies the presence of alternatives". Thus in her discussion of (16)

> (16) Sue won't ever finish her novel, well, Bill thinks.

James say, "it seems that in saying ... <u>well</u> before 'Bill thinks', the speaker is indicating that there are other things he could say in addition to, or instead of, merely saying 'Bill thinks'" (1974:192).

However, James also mentions two other possibilities. <u>Well</u> could indicate merely "reluctance to speak"[3] (<u>ibid</u>. 196):

> (17) I'm afraid John is, well, dead.

or it could indicate that the speaker is "stopping to think about whether to suspend a presupposition", as in

> (18) John doesn't beat his wife anymore, well, if he ever did. (James 1974:189)

But I would claim that these three uses of <u>well</u> are not actually distinct--that in each case <u>well</u> indicates inner consultation and that the differences between these three uses are superficial and transparently related to the contexts in which <u>well</u> is employed.

James places considerable emphasis on the notion of interjectional 'reference'. She takes <u>well</u> in

> (19) The girl who said she liked, well, Vivaldi dried the dishes.

to 'refer' to <u>Vivaldi</u> in the sense that "it is that thing which, while pausing and saying the interjection, the speaker is selecting to mention over other things, trying to think of the best description of, or trying to remember, etc." (1974:113). James sees reference, in this

unusual sense of the word, as a property of pausal interjections she studied and uses the notion to demonstrate
several syntactic restrictions on the use of these forms.
The position taken in the present work is that 'reference' is not a property of interjections, but a pragmatic notion that exists quite independently of them.
The fact that interjections appear to 'refer' to constituents probably just indicates that constituents are units
of utterance planning. Notice that even if an unfilled
pause occurs instead of an interjection, the notion of
'reference' is still applicable:

> (20)   The girl who said she liked...Vivaldi dried
>   the dishes.

The idea that this speaker has stopped to consider the
formulation <u>Vivaldi dried the dishes</u> is just as absurd
here as in the case of (19). The notion of 'reference'
adds nothing to our understanding of the use of <u>well</u>
in particular. The fact that <u>well</u> seems to 'refer' to
what follows rather than what precedes (James 1974:125)
results from the fact that James' internal <u>well</u>'s precede
continuations not corrections (which latter cases James
does not consider). In the case of corrections it is
clear that <u>well</u> is forward-referring only in the sense
that what follows remains to be formulated; in corrections both the correctible and the correction are necessarily involved to some extent in the inner consultation.

4.8   <u>Well</u> and Other-Repair

Goldberg (1980) discusses instances of 'other-repair', such as

> (21)   B: It's very expensive here, I've discovered.
>   A: Yeah(.) Well it would be just as expensive
>   here as in the States, do(n't) you think?
>   (235)

She comments, "When prefaced by a _well_ the speaker of
the other-initiated repair is heard as challenging the
repairable speaker's competence or expertise by indicating that the offered repair is a matter of common
knowledge and that the speaker of the troublesome item
should also share that knowledge" (_ibid_. 234).

Again an understanding of the evincive status of
well can explain why _well_ is used as it is in this particular discourse situation.

The 'challenge' aspect of other-repair with _well_
follows from the fact that _well_ evinces internal consultation following something the other speaker has said.
Since the speaker issuing _well_, if cooperating, is presumed to be mindful of what was just said, to say _well_
just afterward indicates that the speaker wants to be
seen as internally consulting _at this point_. The occasion for this inner consultation inferably involves the
preceding utterance. Notice that even if _well_ alone
is uttered in this position, it can be heard as a challenge:

> (22)　A:　I've known lots of people who've died by
> 　　　　　spontaneous combustion.
> 　　　B:　Well...

B is not only internally consulting but _announces_ that
this is so following another speaker's statement. The
Basic Interpretation Pattern operates to yield a challenge: consideration following a statement by someone
implicates that something about the statement has provoked the speaker's inner consultation. The challenge
is not something inherent in the meaning or use of _well_
but results from applying the usual evincive reading
in yet another discourse environment.

The claim that the offered repair is a matter of
common knowledge is not entirely accurate. The following

exchange seems plausible:

(23) A: A friend of mine had hepatitis.
B: Which kind?
A: It was viral.
B: Well, a doctor friend of mine explained
to me the other day that, contrary to popular belief, both major kinds of hepatitis
are viral.

Here B is clearly not presupposing that the viral nature
of both kinds of hepatitis is common knowledge. Other-
repair this certainly is, however. (Notice that in (21)
the shared knowledge aspect of A's claim is explicitly
indicated by do(n't) you think?)

Goldberg comments on well used in another kind of
repair situation:

Well prefaced acknowledgments of the other's repair
convey a sense of impatience or displeasure. The
other-repair is marked as unwarranted at best and
an uncondonable interruption at worst (Goldberg
1980:240).

She cites the following example:

(24) J: He went right down on the fie:ld'n'e w'js
sittin there talkin like a nigger, en all
the guys (mean) all these niggers er a:ll
// up there in-
R: You mean Ne:gro: don'tcha.
(.)
J: Weh en // there all-ih-u... (ibid. 240)

But is well really the culprit in this tense situation? The scenario: J is speaking; R indicates other-
repair on an item that J considers not to be in need
of repair. B's well (weh) indicates internal consultation regarding what has just occurred--the unwarranted-
seeming repair. Repair in itself, as researchers working
on this subject have found (e.g. Schegloff et al. 1977:
380) is a risky business, however subtly initiated, because it can be the occasion for disagreement. The occurrence of an unwarranted or only questionably warranted

repair can be taken as a 'face threat' of some magnitude. The possibility of impatience or displeasure on the part of J is implicit in the situation itself; the use of well with its ordinary evincive contribution in this situation can suggest that the impatience or displeasure that might arise there in fact has.

Goldberg claims that well in examples like (21) implies acceptance of the correction and she points to a later element in the same exchange to support this claim. The acceptance is probably not a necessary feature of these exchanges. Consider the following:

(25) A: I visited my Aunt Pete.
           B: Do you mean your aunt Greta?
           A: Well, I don't have any Aunt Greta.

Well here could only (indirectly by means of the Basic Interpretation Pattern) indicate acceptance to the extent of having understood and given due consideration to B's question. In general one finds a polite attempt by speakers to see the good in repairs if possible, but it does occur from time to time that a repair is entirely unwarranted, and well does not seem to be excluded in such cases.

4.9 Sentence-final Well

It is frequently pointed out that well is inappropriate sentence-finally:

(26) *My neighbor might wait for me for ten minutes, well. (James 1974:125)

In the evincive treatment, this distributional aspect of well proceeds from the fact that well is predominantly used as an initiator (see Ch. 2). As an evincive initiator (a 'backgrounder') noninternal well's carry the strong implication that something will, or ought to, follow. Pronounced with a corresponding initiatory intonation, (26) becomes acceptable:

(27) My neighbor might wait for me for ten minutes.
Well...

Here the implication is that the speaker is reconsidering
what he or she has just said and considers beginning
(but does not express) a reformulation; whereas, the
speaker of (26) is in the peculiar position of assigning
utterance-final intonation to an item strongly associated
with initiation.

4.10 Reduced Well

Excluding suprasegmental variation, the two principal phonological variants of well are the full form [wEl]
and reduced [wl]. The occurrence of a particular variant
is partly correlated with discourse position: the reduced
variant does not occur as a pausal interjection.

(28) *There were, [wl], four of them.

The reason for this restriction is probably that well
in sentences like (28) is used to embody a genuine pause
for consideration and, if reduced, seems to indicate
that the pause is only perfunctory.

A second interesting restriction is that [wl] preceding a direct answer can be used (via the Basic Interpretation Pattern) to indicate an insufficiency of the
question, but not the inadequacy of the answer:

(29) A: Did you murder your husband?
      B1: [wl] yes.
      B2: Well yes.

Responses B1 and B2 are used differently. B1 would typically be used to convey that the question asked by A
is inappropriate (e.g., because A already knew the answer). B2, on the other hand, is susceptible of this
same 'inappropriateness' interpretation, but also, equal-

ly, of an interpretation in which the answer 'yes' is a qualified one. This difference is, again, probably attributable to the implication involved in using a re-duced variant rather than to something about the meaning of _well_. This distributional restriction follows from an inherent difference between inappropriate questions and insufficient answers. Inappropriateness of a ques-tion is immediately apparent (or, if not, _well_ would not have been used at all). The function of (wḷ) after such a question is to say something like, "Your question has caused me to do a brief double take." The _well_ pre-ceding a considered reply, on the other hand, should, if it is to be taken seriously, be accompanied by a real pause to reflect; the reduced variant would make the inner consultation appear to be mechanical or perfunctory and so undermine the communicative aim of the speaker in uttering it.

4.11 _Well_ and Narrative Elision

Lakoff distinguishes the use of _well_ in narratives to "indicate that details have been omitted, that (the) narrative is not really complete" (1973:464). She cites the following example:

> (30)   ...So the man went to the old witch doctors
>   who lived in each of the pyramids, as he had
>   been instructed. He went to one after another,
>   but none could help him. Finally, he reached
>   the witch doctor who lived in the very last
>   pyramid, and he asked him, 'How can I get the
>   silver screw out of my bellybutton?' _Well_,
>   to make a long story short, the witch doctor
>   who lived in the last pyramid went into his
>   pyramid and came out with a little silver screw-
>   driver. He inserted this in the silver screw
>   that was in the man's bellybutton, and he un-
>   screwed and unscrewed and unscrewed, and fi-
>   nally the screw came out.

Lakoff offers this example (as does Hines 1977) in further support of the claim that <u>well</u> indicates an insufficiency, but the example cannot serve as evidence for this claim because material follows <u>well</u> that explicitly states the narrative has been shortened. Moreover, if <u>well</u> also indicates narrative shortening, (30) should be redundant, but it isn't. Consider another case of initial <u>well</u> in a fabricated narrative:

(31)   ...So what does Bill do? He gets out of the car and says he's going to walk if she won't take him. Well, that's a very long walk, but Bill walked the whole way without looking back once.

Elision is a possible reading of what is going on in (31), but it doesn't seem more likely than various other interpretations. <u>Well</u> could, for example, simply indicate that the speaker is pausing to consider or formulate what he will say next, or could indicate indirectly (via the Basic Interpretation Pattern) that the speaker is beginning an aside to interject subjective material into an otherwise objective narrative account.

Or consider the following fabricated example, for which the elision reading seems remote:

(32)   ...She handed Rob the pancake on a plate and he said, 'but this pancake is GRAY!' He just stared at it with a look of horror on his face. Well, neither of them said a word for about a whole minute or so. Not a muscle moved, and then there's this loud bang from a passing car that backfired...

It is hard to see what <u>could</u> have been elided here, since nothing happened between the moment when Roger began staring at the pancake and the bang out in the street. What is much more likely is that the speaker paused for inner consultation. Of course, if one is pausing in the middle of a narrative, the subject of one's thoughts may well be how to continue or complete the narrative,

or whether to elide certain material, but the particular
reason for the consultation is not expressed by the _well_
itself; it is something known to the speaker but left
to be guessed at or inquired after by the addressee,
or explicated later by the speaker.

4.12 _Well_ and 'Intention'

Murray (1979) has proposed a unifed account of _well_
capable of handling a number of its uses. Murray makes
the following claims (730):

> A. _Well_ signals (draws attention to) some expecta-
>   tion, hope, fear or other nominalization of an
>   intensional verb, to which parties to the dis-
>   course are presumed to have access.
> B. A pragmatic condition is attached to the use
>   of _well_: it is appropriate to use _well_ only
>   if what follows is addressed to the same "inten-
>   sion".

The first claim runs into difficulty in cases like
the following. Consider two people sitting in chairs
in a livingroom reading. One says to the other:

> (33) Well, how do you like that! Microbes are being
>   used to build computers.

This is clearly not a case in which, in Murray's words,
"there is an intension to which parties to the discourse
are supposed to be privy" (731). This _well_ can, however,
be used to indicate that the speaker's statement is based
on internal consultation (here, presumably, reflection
on the reading material).

Discussing how her proposal relates to _well_ preceding answers, Murray claims that "in question answers
well is simply a signal that its speaker is aware of
what some party to the discourse wants to be told" (730).
But _well_ can precede answers to questions the speaker
is unsure of:

(34) A: What are you?
      B: Well, I'm a teacher, if that's what you
          mean.

In the evincive treatment of <u>well</u>, the particle simply
indicates that the speaker is giving a considered reply,
regardless of how well the speaker understands the question.

As further evidence for her claim, Murray cites
the following examples:

(35)
$\{^{Oh}_{*Well}\}$, I've been forgetting to say...

(36)
$\{^{Oh}_{*Well}\}$, by the way...

(37)
$\{^{*Oh}_{Well}\}$, once upon a time...

(38)
$\{^{*Oh}_{Well}\}$, so we'll meet at three...

She comments, "Clearly, only <u>well</u> may introduce an anticipated topic, and only <u>oh</u> a new one". This observation
is correct and consistent with Murray's claims, but does
not support them against the evincive treatment. Oh_1,
by virture of its core contribution (see Ch. 2), is used
before material that just entered the speaker's mind.
The unacceptability of <u>well</u> in (35) and (36) results
from the fact that <u>well</u> indicates current consideration,
which is inconsistent with the unexpected spontaneous
arising of thought. The unacceptability of <u>oh</u> in (37)
and (38) results from the fact that <u>once upon a time</u>
and <u>so we'll meet at three</u> are initiations that would
normally precede material that did not suddenly and spon-
taneously arise in the speaker's mind.

The first of Murray's claims is also problematic
in cases where <u>well</u> seems to draw attention to the nomi-

nalization of an extensional rather than an intensional verb (assuming, for the sake of argument, that it makes sense to speak of <u>well</u> doing such a thing). Consider an exchange like the following:

(39) Could you please state your last two addresses?
Well. I lived at 432 18th, and then at 1604 Canberra.

If <u>well</u> here is spoken with sharply falling intonation (conveying certainty, definiteness), it can be used to signal knowing (<u>know</u>) is factive, not an intensional verb). If <u>well</u> is to be characterized as in Murray's first claim (A above), (39) should be at least mildly contradictory, but it is not. The evincive treatment is, however, straightforwardly applicable to (39): the speaker could be stopping to remember the addresses (with a positive expectation of being able to do so--conveyed by the intonation) and wish to indicate that this is so.

The pragmatic limitation mentioned in Murray's second claim (B above) follows directly from the fact that <u>well</u> is predominantly used as an initiator; as claimed above in Chapter 2, the association of <u>well</u> with initiation is closely related to its status as an evincive.

Thus Murray's proposals are interesting and fairly comprehensive, but all of her examples submit readily to the evincive treatment, and her proposal fails to capture the behavior of <u>well</u> in some environments which the evincive treatment can easily handle.

4.13 Conclusion

The discourse particle <u>well</u> is primarily an evincive indicating consultation by the speaker of his or her current thoughts. This form cannot, therefore, be considered (as in Fries 1952:105) 'meaningless'. The particulars of the consultation evinced by _well_ are not displayed by uttering it, though they may, of course, be elaborated in the speaker's ensuing talk. Inter-sentential _well_ is heard as an initiator (see Ch. 2), based on its usefulness for backgrounding. With its basic evincive use, _well_ serves many secondary discourse functions: introducing questions or answers, direct quotations, topic shifts, exclamations, self- and other-repairs, and so on. In each case the evincive use is primary and the secondary discourse function is a product of applying the Basic Interpretation Pattern to the use of evincive _well_ in particular discourse environments.

The purpose above has not been to discredit the functional approaches to the uses of _well_, which are of interest in themselves, but to provide a unified treatment of _well_ which has the following advantages over previous treatments:

1. It maintains that there is in fact only one discourse particle _well_, rather than a multiplicity of particles _well_ each with a separate discourse function. This treatment is therefore much simpler and more comprehensive than existing treatments.

2. It explains why _well_ in particular gets used for the discourse functions its serves and not for others, and therefore accounts for the item's observed functional 'polysemy'.

An important general feature of the use of _well_ is that it is not used to indicate _all_ internal consultation, but only consultation the speaker wishes to bring up. Many of the functions _well_ may serve depend on the addressee's constructing the speaker's probable reason for bringing up the existence of covert thinking at a given point. Note also that _well_ can be used to indicate current inner consultation of the private world even if no such consultation is actually in progress at the time--that is, _well_ can be used wherever it is only appropriate or desirable to indicate current inner consultation.

A previous attempt to specify the meaning of _well_ by Hines (1977) failed to capture the evincive quality of the item. Hines suggested a link between adverbial _well_ and the discourse particle (see also Sadock 1969: 298), claiming that:

> _well_ is a word with positive connotations. It is used in an evaluative sense as an adverb to indicate a point just above adequacy. When it occurs as an introductory word, it also has positive connotations; it is an affirmation of the right of the previous speaker to say what he says (317).

As implied in 4.5, this affirmative quality of _well_ stems from its use in response to a question, which it indirectly acknowledges. Any real sense of affirmation beyond such acknowledgment evaporates when the item occurs preceding an explicit denial:

(37)   A: Short people should be kept under pool tables.
       B: Well, I hardly think you have the right to say something like that.

There is apparently no current semantic connection whatsoever between adverbial _well_ and evincive _well_.

Consideration of the use of _well_ is complicated by the fact that semantic nuances may be conveyed by the intonation with which the item is spoken. For example, the famed Jack Benny _well_, spoken alone to convey exasperation, is said with rise-fall intonation and breathy voice (literal exasperation). This same meaning could be conveyed by paralinguistic noises uttered with the same intonation and voice quality. This and other special uses of _well_ seem to result from a combination of the evincive use with the separate contribution of intonation and other suprasegmental parameters[4].

Here, as in the discussion of <u>like</u> in Chapter 3, the question of routinization must also be addressed. Has <u>well</u> become conventionalized as the embodiment of the various discourse functions it serves, so that its basic evincive use has been obscured? The contribution of this chapter to an answer to this question has been to estalish that the basic evincive use of the item is respected by all of the separate discourse functions the item can serve. This seems to indicate that the basic use persists and underlies these discourse functions.

CHAPTER FIVE

YOU KNOW

5.1 Preliminary Remarks

The discourse particle <u>you know</u> (hereafter YK)[1], as
in (1)-(3)

    (1) ... if you look YK in the- newspaper ... (RTS,26)
    (2) ... I feel that- YK I think it's wrong ... (RTS,27)
    (3) ... but uh -YK ya get a feeling that ... (RTS,34)

can appear so frequently in conversation that its use by
some speakers is apt to be stigmatized, even by the speakers themselves, as a dysfluency. Others use YK sparingly,
but those who do not use it at all are uncommon, and it is
rare that multi-party talk of any duration fails to contain at least a few instances.

YK is a popular target of prescriptivist railings
against uncommunicative speech. English teachers often
characterize it with epithets like 'verbal garbage' or
'anemic phrase', or to describe YK as a 'crutch' used when
one has nothing to say, or when one cannot, or will not
bother to, find the proper words to express something (cf.
Lomas and Richardson 1956:194-5).[2] These allegations pre-
suppose that YK lacks a specific or important communicative function: YK is seen not as a functional linguistic
item so much as a disfigurement of speech (e.g. Newman
1974:14). Since, however, so many other discourse items
that have been accused of being meaningless (e.g. by Fries
1952:102) have proved on closer examination to be semantically interesting (James 1972, etc.), these accusations
regarding YK are suspicious and provoking.

Probably because it pervades spontaneous talk, a good
deal of scholarly attention has been paid to this item in
various disciplines. By far the most extensive discus-

- 94 -

cussions are in Goldberg 1980, 1981a, 1981b), though that by Bernstein (1962a) is also ambitious. More modest treatments are found in Duncan and Fiske 1977, Jefferson 1972, 1973, Sacks, Schegloff, and Jefferson 1974, and Crystal and Davies 1975. The item is briefly mentioned by numerous other writers.

In this chapter the foregoing treatment of _like_ and _well_ will be extended to include YK; this will require broadening the perspective of the last three chapters, since YK does not lend itself to the evincive treatment accorded _like_ and _well_. In fact, the notion 'evincive' will be seen in this chapter to be only one of a larger set of notions that between them characterize speakers' disclosure activity (see Chapter 1).

The earlier proposals regarding the function of YK will not all be discussed below, though the most substantive of these will all be considered.[3] Sections 5.2 and 5.3 will deal with the differences between YK as a truth parenthetical and as a discourse particle. This distinction is an important one here because only the discourse particle displays properties relevant to disclosure. Sections 5.2, 5.3, 5.4 and 5.6 together will argue for a distinction between exactly two types of YK (in addition to the unremarkable use of YK in sentences such as _You know a lot_). Section 5.5 will propose a core use for the discourse particle YK, and in sections 5.7.1-3, 5.8, 5.9, and 5.10 the core use will be related to the various discourse functions of YK. The notion 'topic tracking' (Goldberg 1980, 1981a), in particular, is criticized at length in 5.7.2. Section 5.11 offers some statistical evidence bearing on the conclusions of this chapter; and 5.12 is a summary and general discussion of the use of YK in conversation.

5.2 YK as a Truth Parenthetical

A sharp distinction can be drawn between two kinds of YK. One is an ordinary truth parenthetical precisely parallel to other truth parentheticals, such as I feel in Max is a Martian, I feel. Sentences containing such parentheticals are commonly thought to be derived from structures in which the main proposition is the embedded complement of the parenthetical. In the analysis proposed by Ross (1973) structures like (4)[4]

(4)

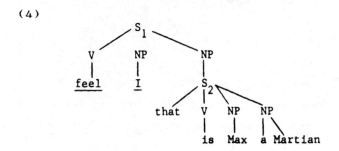

are converted by SLIFTING to structures like (5).

(5)

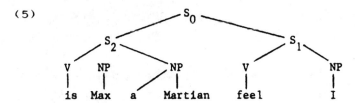

(Parentheticals may also occur within the main sentence in various positions; this is accomplished by NICHING in Ross's analysis.)

A number of diagnostic tests for truth parentheticality are suggested in Knowles 1980; when applied to YK, these clearly indicate that YK, in one use, should be classed with ordinary truth parentheticals. In applying these tests, it is often hard to distinguish the discourse particle from the truth parenthetical. There is, however, a way to avoid the potential ambiguity: only when YK is a truth parenthetical can <u>know</u> be stressed and pronounced with falling intonation. Thus (6) can only have the reading in which the main proposition is understood as the embedded complement of YK:

(6) It's going to be a long evening, y(ou) KNOW.

In applying the following criteria, <u>know</u> will be stressed whenever this would assist the presentation by excluding the irrelevant reading.

5.3 YK and Properties of Truth Parentheticals

In examining the following properties of truth parentheticals as they relate to YK, the intention is not primarily to demonstrate that YK can be used as a truth parenthetical--the first such property is probably sufficient to establish this point. Rather, these properties are presented in order to give a fuller picture of the truth parenthetical use of YK which might, in some cases, assist in distinguishing this use from that in which YK is a discourse particle.

1) <u>Parenthetical verbs</u>. Only certain verbs occur in truth parentheticals (Urmson 1963:220); <u>know</u> is unquestionably one of these:

(7) Gertrude, I know, has no intention of inviting Ezra to tea.
(8) Clyde had, we knew, been to Europe often during the previous four months.

2) <u>Acceptance of Main Clause</u>. Jackendoff (1972) claims that "all the parentheticals are semantically one-place predicates. Exactly one argument is missing, the complement sentence, from the functional structure." Parentheticals must be able to accept the main clause as the missing argument (Knowles 1980:397). This is certainly the case for YK, as indicated by the synonymy of (9) and (10):

(9) John has every intention of being there, you KNOW.
(10) You KNOW John has every intention of being there.

3) <u>Truncated Form</u>. Truth parentheticals are realized by elliptical sentences (i.e. those in which the complement sentence has been elided; this rules out, for example,

(11) *John will eat all the cake, it's true that he will eat cake (Knowles 1980:397).

Likewise ruled out--and, apparently, to the same degree--is

(12) *John will eat all the cake, YK that he will eat cake.

4) <u>Polarity</u>. After an affirmative main clause, truth parentheticals are odd if negative (Knowles 1980: 382):

(13) *John hates all liberated women, it isn't true.

Compare:

(14) *John hates all liberated women, you don't know.

5) <u>Comma Intonation</u>. A truth parenthetical is "set aside intonationally from the intonation contour of the main proposition and has the potential for a slight (comma) pause on either side" (Knowles 1980:381). This is equally true of YK:

(15) Fred...you KNOW...feeds his angelfish only choice brine shrimp.

6) <u>Distribution</u>. Truth parentheticals may be 'niched' into various positions in a sentence. The positions are the same for YK and other truth parentheticals:

(16) John, it's true, went to Paris on Sunday.
John, you KNOW, went to Paris on Sunday.
(17) John went, it's true, to Paris on Sunday.
John went, you know, to Paris on Sunday.
(18) John went to Paris, it's true, on Sunday.

John went to Paris, you know, on Sunday.
(19)   John went to Paris on Sunday, it's true.
John went to Paris on Sunday, you KNOW.

(Know is odd if stressed in (17) and (18); I do not know the reason for this.)

7) Claim to Truth. A declarative truth parenthetical implies a positive claim to the truth of the main proposition[5]:

(20)   *John, it isn't true, had a good time Saturday.

Compare:

(21)   *John, you don't KNOW, had a good time Saturday.

8) Occurence After Imperatives. In general truth parentheticals cannot occur after imperatives (cf. Knowles 1980:402):

(22)   *Get out of my way, { it's true. / I expect. }

Compare:

(23)   *Get out of my way, you KNOW.

5.4   Evidence for Two Types of YK

In an early presentation of her ideas, Goldberg (1976) argues for three types of YK. It will be argued here that there are in fact only two clearly distinct types, which will be referred to as YKa and YKb. In this section some potential evidence for such a two-way distinction will be considered.

Goldberg (1976:14) cites examples such as (24) in which YK has its full literal meaning, and the sentence is not acceptable:

(24)   *YK that Harry is an idiot is believed by Martha.

Compare:

(25)   YK, that Harry is an idiot is believed by Martha.

Goldberg explains the unacceptability of (24) as follows: "When a sentence is embedded in an island, it cannot easily contain the primary information the speaker is interested in conveying to his addressee" (1976:14). Probably the explanation for the unacceptability of (24) is simpler though: subject complements require a complementizer, which is lacking here. The sentence becomes acceptable with the addition of <u>that</u>:

    (26)   That you know that Harry is an idiot is believed
            by Martha.

YK is not part of the subject complement in (25) and is therefore not ruled out.

      Certain tagged sentences may be cited as evidence for a distinction between two types of YK:

    (27) YK Alice is a sharp tens player, don't you?
    (28) *YK, Alice is a sharp tens player, don't you?

As Goldberg (1976:28) points out in regard to similar sentences, the unacceptability results because <u>don't you?</u> requires an antecedent in the main proposition, but only in sentences like (27) is an antecedent present. This is not, of course, evidence for a difference between truth parenthetical YK and the discourse particle, since in (27) YK is not parenthetical at all, and in fact (27) becomes unacceptable if there is a comma pause after YK. (Oddly, in Goldberg's examples parallel to (27) a comma follows YK; that is why other examples are used here.)

      A third example cited by Goldberg (1976:23) involves indirect speech acts:

    (29)   YK it's cold in here.
    (30)   YK, it's cold in here.

Only (30), she claims, can be used to perform an indirect speech act. Probably the claim should be that (29) can embody a more forceful indirect speech act than (30). Notice that (31) can serve to make a very pointed indirect request:

(31) YK (that) I like salt on my potatoes.

(32) can also convey an indirect request, though a more polite one:

(32) YK, I like salt on my potatoes.

In terms of the typology of levels of directness proposed in House and Kasper 1981:163-4, (32) ranks only as a 'strong hint', while (31) is more direct in that it "asserts a preparatory condition holding for the execution of the action".

Goldberg claims (1976:25) that YK in sentences like (29) does not necessarily imply that "the speaker believes or knows the proposition to hold. (This use of YK) literally claims only that the addressee does know the proposition... If on the other hand a speaker uses (the discourse particle YK, as in (30)], the speaker himself must know or believe in the proposition." No examples are cited, but if this claim is applied straightforwardly to examples like (33) and (34), its truth is doubtful:

(33) YK John will come if you ask him to.
(34) YK, John will come if you ask him to.

My strong intuition is that (33) does indeed imply that the speaker believes that John will come if asked. I do, however, agree with Goldberg's assessment that (34) makes a stronger claim about an addressee's knowledge than does (34).

The arguments in Goldberg (1976) favoring a distinction between two types of YK are suggestive, but this distinction only emerges clearly when the core use of YKb is considered.

5.5 The Use of YKb

Goldberg (1976:42) suggests as a rough synonym for the discourse particle YK, 'you know what I'm talking about'. Other near paraphrases are possible--some nearer than others:

(41)

$$
(you) \left\{ \begin{array}{l} \begin{Bmatrix} understand \\ dig_6 \\ see \\ understand \end{Bmatrix} ? \\ \begin{Bmatrix} get \\ hear \\ follow \\ dig \\ see \end{Bmatrix} \quad what \ I \ \begin{Bmatrix} mean \\ 'm \ saying \end{Bmatrix} ? \end{array} \right.
$$

These all have in common that the speaker is questioning whether what is said has been correctly understood by some other(s). Notice that the verb <u>know</u> in one sense means 'understand' or 'grasp', as in

(42)   I know how sewing machines work.

Ignoring for the moment the difference between interrogative and declarative YKb, I would like to propose the following core use for YKb in all of its situations of occurence:

> YKb indicates that the speaker expects that there is no communicatively significant discrepency between what is now in the private world and what is now in the other world, with respect to what is now in the shared world.

This proposed use is not, in broad outline, anything particularly new. It is fairly close to Goldberg's 'you know what I'm talking about' and to other loose characterizations (e.g. in Labov and Fanshel 1977; Crystal and Davy 1975; Lakoff 1974; Bernstein 1962b; Fowler 1978); the proposed 'definition' is, however, quite specific in the way it relates the use of YKb to the problem of disclosure (see Ch. 1), and some initial justification for this treatment will now be offerred.

First note that the proposed use provides an explanation for the odd fact that YKb cannot occur after true questions:

(43)   *Who are you, YK?
(44)   *What time is it, YK?

The anomaly results because a true question seeks information from some other(s), while, according to the proposed use, YKb presumes a fundamental correspondence between what is in the private world and what is in the other world.   Notice that YKb is perfectly acceptable after rhetorical questions, in which the speaker is not really seeking information:

(45)   The first thing I did after I inherited the billion was walk into my local Rolls dealer and say, "Give me four of the yellow ones". The guy looked at me funny and said, "Are you sure about that?" I said, "Sure I'm sure." I mean, what's a Rolls cost, YK?

The proposed use also explains why YKb cannot occur with certain conversational items:

(46)   *Hello, YK(?)[7]
       *Oh hell, YK(?)
       *Bye now, YK(?)
       *Oops, YK(?)

In these cases the speaker uses routine items that are so transparent in use or meaning that it would be peculiar for the speaker to be interested in affirming that they have been properly appreciated.

Statements about the speaker's personal thoughts or feelings which an addressee could not be aware of provide an interesting perspective on the use of YKb. Consider the following sentences:

(47)   I feel a chill, YK?
(48)   I was born in Brooklyn, YK?
(49)   I disagree with you, YK?

YKb is only appropriate in these cases when there is some

'room for agreement' between the private and other worlds; what the agreement is differs according to details of the sentence to which YK is attached. Thus in (47) the speaker could be asking if the addressee is _also_ chilled and therefore able to appreciate _I feel a chill_--or whether the addressee is familiar with the sensation of feeling a chill. Suppose, for the sake of argument, that in (48) the speaker conveys information the addressee was not aware of. An answer of "Yeah, I have a grandmother who lives there" would be an appropriate response in that it acknowledges some shared ground between the private and other worlds with respect to what has been said. Although in (49) a correspondence between private and other worlds is specifically denied in the main proposition, the sentence is nevertheless acceptable with YKb if the particle is taken to imply something like, "We share a basic understanding of my motive for disagreeing". Thus application of the proposed use of YKb in different contexts has strikingly different results.

Although YKb expects a correspondence between the private and other worlds, it is used in cases of uncertainty about that correspondence: if there were no such uncertainty, there would be no point in mentioning the presumed correspondence. This uncertainty can be concerning something connected with the sentence in which YKb occurs, for example, an awkwardness of expression:

(50)   For our ducks we had them install a sort of
        largish pool-like thing, YK?

(cf. 5.7.3 below on the use of YKb at repair sites). Or the uncertainty can be occasioned by a possible difficulty in appreciating the sequential relevance of the item with which YKb occurs. Assume that the speakers in the following exchange are acting cooperatively and that they are strangers passing each other on the sidewalk:

(51) A: Excuse me. Do you have the time?
      B: It's six o'clock, YK.

YKb is odd here because there is nothing apparently problematic about B's utterance given its context, so that it is odd for B to bring up the existence of a possible discrepency between the private and other worlds. But as part of a narrative, B's YKb tagged utterance can become acceptable when there is conceivably some difficulty for an addressee in appreciating the sequential relevance of the statement:

(52) So Baby Face turns the dial and listens to the tumblers with his fingers. A light goes on outside the bank, but it's only a streetlight. It's six o'clock, YK.

The speaker in this hypothetical example wishes to confirm that the addressee has caught the significance of <u>it's six o'clock</u> with respect to the fact that the streetlight went on. Notice that it is not the propositional content of the sentence <u>it's six o'clock</u> that is at issue here, so that it would be incorrect to say that YKb checks to see if speaker and addressee are together with regard to the propositional content of the utterance; rather, it is the sequential relevance of <u>it's six o'clock</u> that matters.

In the following sections it will be assumed that the use of YKb is that proposed above and that the only difference between the declarative and interrogative uses is their declarativity versus interrogativity (though the interrogative is discussed separately in 5.9). Note that YKb tentatively posits <u>some</u> area of speaker/addressee solidarity with respect to the sentence to which YKb is attached, but that the basis of this solidarity can vary greatly from case to case.

- 106 -

5.6 A third YK?

There appears to be no substantive difference between Goldberg's YK II (=YKb) and her YK III. She assigns to the third category instances of YK in positions of hesitation, as in (54),

(53) I have some...YK...salami in my room if you'd like some. (Goldberg 1976:8)

claiming there are two differences between types II and III, and that the second of these differences is crucial for distinguishing the two types:

i) <u>Pause length</u>. YK II is "embedded in pauses of perceptually longer duration than the normal juncture pauses of [types I and II]" (48).
ii) <u>Distribution</u>. "<u>Y'know</u> III as a filled pause can occur in syntactic environments prohibited to <u>y'know</u> I and II" (49).

The first of these differences does seem insufficient to distinguish the two types, but the second difference is insufficient also. The data given in support of the syntactic restrictions are:

(54) a. *any, you know, peas
     b. *any, y'know, peas
     c. any...you know...peas

I find (54a-c) all acceptable. But my objection goes beyond this intutitive disagreement: it is circular to claim a distinction between II and III and then, as the only evidence for the distinction, cite cases where III occurs but II does not. This presupposes the distinction being argued for.

The position taken here is that YK III is really just YKb used in a position of interjection (a matter of where, rather than what). Since YKb is structurally independent of the main sentence,it is not surprising that it can fit into virtually any slot in a sentence.[8] A hesitation pause can accomodate YKb as well as the beginning or end of a sentence can. There is no fundamental difference in the use of YK between cases of YK II and putative cases of YK III; the use proposed above for YKb is suitable in both cases, except that in the hesitation cases YKb is interpreted in the context of a pause before some item next to be spoken. This use of YKb is discussed more fully below.

5.7 Discourse Functions of YKb

In the next several sections it will be shown how the discourse functions of YKb follow from the proposed core use of the particle. As in the previous two chpaters, the claim will be that there is an underlying unity in all uses of this item and that functional differences arise when the item is used in particular discourse contexts. As is true for like and well, the core use of YKb naturally results in the item's having multiple functions.

5.7.1 Topic Introduction

Goldberg (1980, 1981b) notes the frequent occurrence of YK before the introduction of a new topic, as in (55):

(55) President Nixon is talking to John Dean. Dean has just entered the room.

P: Hi John, how are you?
D: Good morning. Good morning.
P: Sit down. Sit down. Trying to get my remarks ready to (unintelligible) the building trades.
D: So I understand.
P: Yes, indeed, yeah. You know, I was thinking we ought to get the odds and ends, uh (unintelligible) we talked, and, uh, it was confirmed that--you remember we talked about resignations and so forth and so on--that I should have in hand, not to be released.
                    (White House:16-4-73am:187)
                    (Cit. in Goldberg 1980:96)

She notes that topic introduction is problematic because it is 'face-threatening':

The speaker who initiates a new topic before the ongoing topic has been terminated can be regarded as threatening the other's face by suggesting that what the other is saying is of no interest to the speaker or, if the speaker interrupts himself then he can be heard as saying that what was being said is not intended for the other to hear. Similarly, if after the ongoing talk has reached a successful end a new topic is initiated but fails to receive the other's support, then the speaker who initiated the new topic is subject to a face threat (Goldberg 1981b:3).

YK used to introduce a new topic, it is claimed, serves to aleviate the face-threatening potential of an obvious and abrupt topic change:

A strategy most often employed to this end is to go even more baldly on record as initiating a topic change. Bounded topic initiation is blatant at the best of times so why not carry this property to its extreme: call attention to it, notify the addressees that this is the speaker's intent (Goldberg 1981b:5).

On this view YK is considered one of a set of items referred to as 'disjunct markers' the function of which is to flag initiating utterance-units. Other members of this set are hey, oh (i.e. oh_1; see 2.2 above), by the way, speaking of, guess what, vocatives, etc.

This analysis is a later development of ideas in Goldberg 1980, where it is reported that 73% of YK marked moves in the corpora used for that study are '(re-)introducing moves'. This statistic does not by itself establish the role of YK as a topic introducer. The 73% figure is not compared to the overall frequencies of all move types in the data and is uninterpretable in isolation.

The claim in Goldberg 1980 that YK is a 'marker' of introducing moves is replaced in a later analysis (Goldberg 1981b) by the 'disjunct marker' approach. As implied in the second quotation above, it is difficult to regard YK as marking introduction because bounded topic changes are themselves "blatant"; moreover, they are usually prefaced by a facilitating pause. Between these two indications of topic change, it would be unnecessary to mark initiation itself. It remains superficially reasonable, though, to claim that YK prefacing a topic change somehow calls attention to the change and so, by a strange twist, undercuts the possible face threats involved in the change by pointing to it. The supposed effect, in this view, would be parallel to that obtained by saying, "You might think this rude of me, but..." It is clear from Goldberg's numerous examples that YKb is particularly at home before topic initiations/changes. Her characterization of YK as "possibly the least obtrusive and disruptive" of the disjunctive items also seems to me to be correct.

The approach to be taken here to this use of YKb is to claim that the particle, by virtue of its core use, receives a special interpretation in pre-topical discourse position which makes it particularly useful in that position.

All utterance-initial uses of YKb have a general peculiarity. With the proposed use YKb presumes some shared ground between the private and other worlds with respect to what is in the shared world; but initial YKb posits this presumed correspondence _before_ the utterance in question has in fact been spoken into the shared world. The placement of YK in pre-topical position with its basic use amounts to a _prediction_ of common ground. As such, YKb in this position can be considered a type of 'intimacy ploy' (for this term see Schegloff 1968:1078). It is as if the speaker were saying, "We trust each other; our sensibilities are so attuned that I can count on your appreciation of esentials of what I say even before I say it". This peculiarity of initial YKb no doubt explains why the item carries a sense of 'folksiness'. Newman seems more or less on target when he notes (1975:28) that initial YK used in television commercials conveys "that the person doing the commercial is down to earth, regular, not stuck up, and therefore to be trusted."[9]

This use of YKb asserts the existence of a shared orientation from the outset, which then buffers the introduction of new material. We thus have, in the use of YKb here with its proposed core contribution, an underlying reason for why YKb performs topic initiations that are, in Goldberg's terms, "not obtrusive and disruptive".

It is thus again possible to use the discourse context in conjunction with a particle's core use to account for one of its special functions. In the present case, the relevant position of YKb is between two utterances that are topically disjoint, or else before the first topic. With its basic use YKb asserts an overriding continuity despite the obvious topical discontinuity. The item does not exaggerate the discontinuity, as Goldberg claims, but attenuates it by asserting that a shared understanding spans the topical switch: 'You can understand, comfortably encompass, go along with, my current act of topic changing/initating'. There is some truth in the notion that the speaker of YKb in this position is "baldly" annoucning the topic initiation. By asserting continuity of understanding, the speaker does implicate the existence of discontinuity; the real force of YKb here, though, is not to exaggerate the discontinuity but to play it down.

5.7.2 Topic Tracking

Goldberg (1980, 1981a) argues extensively that YK can be used as a 'topic tracking device' "optimally employed, in English, for indicating the central line of development or other important, noteworthy items" in extended talk by a speaker (1980:142). It is specifically those YKs not used (solely) for repair that are thought to have this property (143). Topic tracking YKs are thought to tag: i) topically significant items; ii) repetitions of topically significant items; and iii) parallel structures or contrastive items in the presentation of the topic talk. The function of topic tracking is to clarify which items are 'on' the topical core and distinguish them from items 'off' the core. This is seen as necessary because "items which are off the main line of development may inadvertently pull the talk onto tangential topics" (145). The function of topic tracking is therefore to prevent these "potential drifts" (147) and also to prevent topics being subsumed by other topics (167). Determination of what is on and off the core is conducted by an algorithm details of which will not be discussed here (see Goldberg 1980) since they do not bear directly on the present arguments.

In written language, indications of topical value are "usually accomplished...by grammatical subordination, relativization, and pronominalization" (Goldberg 1980:148), but in unplanned conversation, topic tracking with YK is thought to predominate (149); reiterations are also used, though to a lesser extent (150-156).

The claim that "free-floating" YKs tag topical value is a strong one, as Goldberg is aware, and cannot be adequately supported simply by citing examples. In this connection, the following qualification is important:

> This tracking account of y'know has the status of a description rather than an explanation. Support for this account comes in the form of examples... Of course, given that the tagging of topically significant items is optional, the descriptive account itself is in danger of being vacuous. Until a stronger account is offered, the one I have proposed seems reasonable (Goldberg 1980:168-169).

In the remainder of this section several arguments will be given to show that there us currently no evidence that YK is in fact a topic tracking device and that the notion should be abandoned. These arguments are summarized in the following list, then discussed separately:

1) <u>Simpler alternatives to topic tracking (TT) exist</u>. TT is not the most straightforward account of the occurence of "free floating" YK's;

2) <u>TT is excessively powerful</u>. The range of possible TT points is too unconstrained; almost anything can, in some interpretation, be considered topically significant;

3) <u>TT lacks distributional accountability</u>. TT offers no account of the diversity of placement positions of YK within utterances;

4) <u>TT lacks positive support</u>. TT is not unambiguously supported by existing data;

5) <u>Counterexamples to TT exist</u>. Clear cases of YK attached to utterances off the topical core occur frequently;

6) <u>A unifed approach to YK is possible</u>. An account is proposed that faciitates inclusion of all instances of YKb within a single adequate description.

1. <u>Simpler alternatives</u>. Consider an extended example. The following passage used by Goldberg (1980:163-4) to exemplify TT is from a transcript appearing in Sharrock and Turner 1978:190-6.

```
(56)  C:  I ha:ve a complaint um my neighbor is (0.5)
          le- subl- well renting her garage out, and ah
          there are young boys, now they seem awfully
          nice an' everything but I don't know they're
          missing an awful lot of school, they're fif-
          teen-year-old types, (0.5) an, they've got,
          apparently they've got seven old cars, I guess
          they buy these old cars, but about a month
          ago they went to town sma:shing one of them
          ewith a pick axe ju:st absolutely annoying
        1>you know  pounding all day,=
      P:  (Mm)
      C:  But anyway there is two more cars in the--eh
```

- 113 -

```
        garage now: and--ah, the neighbor works in
        fact she's away all day 'n' she doesn't know
        what's going on but these kids are just
        spending their (h-e) one particular is spend-
        ing most of the day there, and I know::? that
        he's taking parts like driveshaft I-I just
        saw the muffler going with him just now?,
        (0.5) They take them an' we live close by,
        it's in (( section of Newton )) Willow
        Heights an' it's by Gullypark; an' they take
     2›these (1.0) you know, big enough parts to
        ca:rry an' I: think they're dumping them into
        the gully; (1.0) and I'm just getting a lit-
     3›tle, annoyed about it because e--ah you know
        I I think they've got about seven cars, I
        talked to one of the boys and I didn't let on
     4›that I was you know (1.0) annoyed or anything
        but and I wasn't at the//time,
P:      Do these cars all got license on them lady?
C:      A::h, e they're in a garage; I don't
        know that.
P:      What is your name please.
C:      Ah my name is Missis Tho:mpson, and it's at
        her address is twenty-nine thirty-four west
        thirty-four.
P:      Thirty-nine,
C:      No twenty-nine twenty-fi-- ah twen-- ((ra-
        pidly)) I'm twenty-nine twenty-five.  Twenty-
        nine, thirty-four (1.0) west thirty-//four
P:      West thirty--four, (that's)=
C:5›= An' they're taking, you know these pa:rts,
        an' my daughter, (I got) a ten-year-old, was
        saying that she's seen all sorts of these
        parts down at the gully, I guess they go they
        follow the la:ne east, (its inna) into the
        next blo:ck, and whether they're dumping or
        assembling something down there I really
        don't know but-- (1.0) ( i-e) they're sorta
        taking over the area with this business of
     6›eyou know, (        sma//shing up these
        things,=
P:      ( repairing )
C:      =an' I know it's their business if their dads
        allow them to do it but (0.5) they're not
        they're not doing it by their house they've
        they live further down this one particular I
        know where he lives 'n' ah (...)
```

In every case in this passage (and, in fact, in all of
Goldberg's putative examples of TT), the appearance of YKb

can be explained on other grounds having to do with the particular discourse context in which the item appears and the basic use of YKb. It is therefore not necessary to include TT (at least with YK) as part of communicative competence.

In example (56) YK#1, in accordance with its core use, 'presumes' that the addressee (a police officer) grasps the speaker's intent. To understand the placement of YKb in this passage, it is important to keep in mind the nature of the telephone call: a complaint to the police. It is crucial that one who wishes to be heard as issuing a legitimate complaint establish that some law has been violated, or may well have been violated. It is equally important to the complainer that the call not be heard as a mere 'gripe', based solely on personal ill will toward the parties complained against. In this particular complaint call the caller repeatedly (see the full text of the call in Sharrock and Turner 1978) allows the call to appear to be a gripe and moves to correct this impression, or talks in ways obviously geared to forestall the conclusion that the call is a gripe. Immediately before YK#1, the caller used the word annoying, and, immediately following #1, pounding. Annoying is a gripe word, which gets replaced with a factual description: pounding all day. Pounding all day is a substitution which is also a grammatical continuation. YKb is thus at a repair site. Despite the absence of pauses, which, for Goldberg, are criterial for determining where repair occurs, the occurrence of a repair here is obvious. (Moreover, it is not clear that there is no pause, since in this transcript only longish pauses are noted, and these are only grossly indicated.)

YK#2 is also at a repair site. This in indicated both by the one-second pause preceding YK and by the dis-

continuity of the utterance when YK#2 is removed (_an'_
they take these big enough parts). It is reasonable
to suppose that the speaker cannot think of a smooth continuation of the utterance having begun it with _they take_
these and pauses before settling for the awkward _big_
enough parts to carry (awkward both because it doesn't fit
well after _these_ and because it doesn't make especially
good sense--Are some parts _not_ big enough to carry?).

YK#3 is similar. Whatever the transcription _e--ah_
is intended to convey phonetically, it seems clear that
the speaker is experiencing a dysfluency. Notice that
here again the speaker is shifting from personal annoy-
ance to a factual description: _I think they've got about_
seven cars. The reason for the break in continuity is
probably that the caller is 'changing gears'--_I think..._,
after all, stands better as a reformulation than a continuation of the clause introduced by _because_.

YK#4 is also at a trouble spot. The caller has previously retracted _annoy_ twice, if the instance at #3 is
counted, and here pauses a full second before issuing the
retracted word. Notice that _annoy_ is followed immediately
by a 'downgrader' (see House and Kasper 1981:166) which
lessens its force. The speaker is transparently involved
in repair.

YK#5 is another instance of the recurrence of a
trouble source. The same trouble that occurred at #2 occurs here again. This time the abbreviated _these pa:rts_
chosen. This is not an instance of repair but of the introduction of a difficult designation (and, simultaneously, reintroduction of the earlier topic). The core use of
YKb is reasonable here: the caller has previously described these parts (after YK#2) and can be taken as
pointing to the shared ground already established between
speaker and addressee.

YK#6 is at a repair site. Whatever _eyou_ indicates
phonetically, it is clear that some kind of discontinuity
has occurred--a hesitation noise interrupted by YK or some
word cut off by YK. And, again, the site is a delicate
one at which it is important to establish the factual basis of the complaint. (It may be relevant that the police
officer initiates other-repair on what the caller formu-
lates.)

It can be argued, then, that these instances of YK
all occur at points of difficulty of one kind or another
and that it is therefore not necessary to resort to TT
to explain their occurrence. There is some posititve indication of difficulty, discontinuity, or outright repair
at the site of each YK in the passage, and since YKb is
common at repair sites in general, and there has its usual core use (see 5.7.3), TT lacks appeal. This passage is
only one of several cited by Goldberg; the others also
submit readily to reanalysis based on the core use of YKb.

2. Excessive Power. The TT analysis is viable only
if 'topic' can be defined in a way that permits uncontro-
versial assignment of utterances to topics; the analysis
also requires some way to distinguish more important
utterances within a particular topic from those that are
less important. The problem that arises here is that when
these notions are applied intuitively--as they generally
are (especially the latter one)--there is a methodological
danger that the utterances viewed as topically important
will be taken, circularly, to be those tagged by YK. Indeed, it is only via much stretching of the original simple TT idea that certain stray YKb's can be brought into
the TT fold. Not only are 'global topics' considered to
be (optionally) so marked, but so are 'local topics',
'sublocal topics', and utterances that tie local to global
and local to sublocal topics (Goldberg 1980:147;183).

Instances of YK not immediately classifiable as marking topical value can often be conveniently shunted into the repair category. Goldberg claims, "when a repairable or repaired item _is_ a significant item of a passage, the tracking usage of the particle may combine with the repair usage." But how is this possible? If YK in these cases serves to track the topic, there must be some way to tell a tracking repair from a nontracking one. The only way to do this is to appeal to some a priori notion of topical significance, but if this is done, the TT notion is vacuous. This raises an embarrassing question: If an analyst can determine what is topically significant independent of the YK tag (which is Goldberg's claim) <u>why cannot addressees do the same thing</u>?

3. <u>Distributional Accountability</u>. The TT analysis offers no explanation for the fact that YKb can appear at various positions within an utterance with different effects. All placements are regarded as functionally equivalent in that they mark the utterance as one of topical significance. With its core use, however, YKb can function to indicate that the speaker presumes addressee-speaker solidarity with respect to part of an utterance, or even more than one part:

(57)   I YK sort of budged the YK root-looking thing
       into my - YK whatchacallit - Cusinart! - and ran
       like hell.

YKb in such cases is essentially forward-looking (cf. Goldberg 1980:105).

4. <u>Lack of Positive Evidence</u>. As Goldberg concedes, citing possible examples cannot clinch the case for TT. There are two separate problems here:

i) Examples would have to be chosen randomly or considered exhaustively within a large corpus to be of conclusive value to the claim; and the examples would have to be unambiguous between TT and repair;

- 118 -

ii) the TT function implies that addressees are able to reconstruct the topical value of YK tagged utterances within a topic independent of the content and sequential placement of the utterances; some positive evidence that they do so is required. If addressees do not use YKb to track topics, the TT notion is of no demonstrated communicative importance.

     5. <u>Counterexamples</u>. According to the TT hypothesis, it should not be possible to find YKb marked utterances which are both 1) off the topical core and 2) not at a repair site. Goldberg considers off the topical core utterances that "provide more background to an understanding of (some previous item)" (1980:145). Thus she considers the fifth sentence in the following passage to be off-core:

> (58)   I discovered that the mother mouse wasn't in the cage. She just wasn't there. She had been there the day before. She was so big that she couldn't easily get through the bars of the case. <u>She was big because she had just had two litters</u>. Her absence was, therefore, very odd. (Goldberg 1980:144; underscoring mine)[10]

In (60)-(62) below are presented three cases from a single LAB conversation in which YKb occurs with an utterance which, in just this way, provides background to an understanding of previous talk by the same speaker.

> (59)   EVA: She goes in there she goes - "Fanny!" (<-loud whisper) and she was tryin(g) to <u>do</u> it without wakin(g) up Janice cuz Janice hadn't got up yet YK - and she just tries wakin(g) her up and wakin(g) her up and she just raises up (h)er head - and she looks at (h)er and she just passes out again.
>
> (60)   EVA: And I don't remember that- I don't remember- Charlie callin(g) me I forgot he did call me that day but I had forgotten about it an(d) I <u>know</u> he would never change (it) charge it ta anyone else's number

```
SUE:     Yeah
           (
EVA:      because YK he just pays for it automati-
          cally.  And I said "Well I don't remember
          gettin(g) any phone calls" an(d) I said
          "and I'm the only one that's even near
          Dayton" I said "so I'm sure the phone call
          would've been for me"...
(61)  SUE:  Are you gonna sublet yours?
      EVA:  We're gonna. I dunno. Janice was talkin(g)
          about gettin(g) a job down here - nex(t)
          summer
           (
      SUE:  Yeah:::.  That could be because-
      EVA:  Carla (was-) wants to too and (I-) and well
          like Ron's goin(g) ta school this summer so
          she might go the nex(t) summer too cuz
          she's engaged an(d) I'm sure she wants ta
          get out as soon as possible YK
                                        (
      SUE:                            Yeah.
```

6. <u>A unified Approach</u>. The proposed use of YKb can
be applied to explain the occurrence of YKb wherever it is
found in conversation. There is no evidence for a split
between two categories: repair and nonrepair.

It is certainly true that YKb often occurs with topically significant utterances in a conversation. With its
basic use YKb is suitable for checking (with a positive
expectation) whether speaker and addressee are 'on the
same track'. It stands to reason that speakers might be
particularly likely to perform such checking at points
where to do so is most crucial--when a misunderstanding
would have the most detrimental effect on communication.
Key points in topical talk might thus be expected to be
statistically very likely to co-occur with YKb--but so
might, for example, utterances that are awkward or odd in
some way. The speaker is simply checking to see how s/he
is doing at points where this seems to him or her to
matter. It is a rather long step--both experimentaly and
theoretically--from this simple claim to the idea that

YK's are used and understood as markers of topical importance.

5.7.3 YKb and Repair

There is now an extensive literature on conversational repair (e.g. Jefferson 1972, 1974; Schegloff et
al. 1977, Schegloff 1978; DuBois 1974; Goodwin 1975;
Shimanoff and Brunak 1977). YKb occurs frequently at
sites of self-repair. In Goldberg (1980) it is argued
that YK is a 'marker' of self-repair in examples like the
following (repair site underlined):

(62)   Chuck, Chuck <u>has gone through, you know, has
       worked on the list</u>, and Dean's working the, the
       thing through IRS and, uh, in some cases, I
       think, some other (-----) things.
                         [White House:15-9-72:1]
                         (Cit. by Goldberg 1980:216)
(63)   A: Well, then in two weeks there's his birthday
            which comes out on a Saturday night. So
            <u>we'll probably, y'know, maybe we'll</u> do some-
            thing then, =
                         [S/S: Arrangements:201]
                         (Cit. by Goldberg 1980:218)

In self-correction the speaker of some repairable executes
repair on it (to be contrasted with other-repair in which
the speaker performs repair on another's utterance). The
reader is referred to the studies mentioned above for details on repair and correction. Familiarity with these
studies will not be assumed below.

In Goldberg (1980) a sharp distinction is drawn between TT YK and the repair marker. Three differences are
found to obtain between the two types:

i)   repair YK's are not confined to clausal or
       phrasal boundaries, but repair TT YK's are;

ii)   repair YK's are "preceded by (and may be followed
       by) a 'noticed' pause of a microsecond or
       longer";

iii) the pronoun of repair YK's tends to be heard as lightly stressed, while that of the TT use is heard as elided.

The first 'difference' cannot be considered criterial for distinguishing the two types. The distinction is circularly presupposed and then used to support the distributional difference. The second difference is likewise dependent on the proposed distinction itself; moreover, YK's used at repair sites needn't always be preceded by a noticeable pause (the figure of one microsecond is puzzling since most of the transcripts Goldberg uses are not annotated with precise pause measurements). There is, for example, no noticeable pause in the following examples:

(64) C: ... after it's been YK after the person's been shot ... (RTS,99)
(65) C: ... I think that's YK I think we should do that ... (RTS,131)

The third difference is difficult to interpret. Is a real articulatory/acoustical difference referred to or not? In either case the distinction is dubious. The transcripts for the present study abound with apparent counterexamples in which YKb at a repair site seems to this writer to lack any perceptible stress on you.

YKb at repair sites appears not to be substantially different from instances of YKb elsewhere.

In Goldberg's treatment YK at repair sites indicates "that a repair has been initiated (which tends) to occur in the same turn as the trouble-source" (1980:214). The repairs marked by YK "tend to clarify person, event, time, place, and other types of information. The repair upgrades the item's specificity" (217). The tendency for such repairs to "clarify" is, of course, an implicit feature of most all repair (otherwise why repair?), and the claim that repairs involving YK upgrade specificity is likewise very general. Since most repairs involve some kind of reattempt or reformulation, one is free to claim that such repairs result in a more specific rendering of what the speaker first said or intended to say. The claim, though valid, is, however, not very illuminating. Why does YK often accompany repairs that result in greater specificity?

Note that YKb cannot very appropriately be used in cases where the repair involves radical changes like that in (66):

(66) ?I got a dog YK cat for my birthday.

though I mean goes well here. The apparent reason for this is that it is unlikely that the addressee could grasp the speaker's intention (cat) from that speaker's having said dog, without further context or foreknowledge. YKb is much better suited to repairs of the following type:

(68) I had to turn ... YK swerve to avoid the truck. (RTS,1)

where swerve is a plausible and inferable intention of the speaker in saying turn, or to similar cases like (69)

(69) They have nice dresses in there. They may not be nice - YK like - so nice but they have nice dresses. (LAB-A,8)

More radical changes like that from dog to cat in (66) seem better served by particles that explain the substitution, rather than, as YKb does, appealing to the addressee's own ability to grasp the intended meaning. The correct generalization seems to be that YKb, as may be expected from its core use, can appear in repair sites where the speaker wishes to affirm that an addressee understands what is meant. In particular cases this will involve uncertainty as to the obviousness of the speaker's intention in uttering the repairable, or of the speaker's reason for repairing, of the suitability of a particular repair, etc. To asign YK an invariable repair marking function misses the fact that the core use permits multiple functions according to context.

Goldberg makes the interesting comment that some YK marked repairs are 'semi-overt' (cf. DuBois 1974:III-5) in the sense that in these cases the repairable is "detected and deleted before it is vocalized but the YK marker is not" (Goldberg 1980:215). She cites (70) as an example of this:

(70) Well, it's just none of their- you know, that's
      really none of their business. (White House:28-
      2-73:43)

Goldberg's claim here is that the complete repair structure is X-YK-X' and she speculates that cases of 'semiovert' repair "may have prompted the labeling of YK as a 'hesitation marker'".

The issue of. whether or not YK can appear in positions of hesitation (versus instances of correction) hinges on whether or not examples can be found in which YK flanked by one or two pauses appears clause internally where no correction is evident--for example in the case of a word search. Such examples are not hard to find:

(71) C: ... an employee should be able to evaluate
          - and his abilities as a manager - and uh -
          YK time manager etcetera (RTS,1)
(72) And the/n/ one of them is..playing like with
      (.4) I don't remember, I used to play with /it/
      when I was a kid, (.9 but (.75)) it's like a..
      wooden paddle (.6(.3) that (.15)) there's an
      elastic string attached to and there's a ball,
      (.3) you know that kind of thing that you (.4)
      you (.15) I..don't remember the name of them (.35)
      but I played /with them/ for hours. (Chafe 1980:
      309)

With its ordinary use YKb is suitable for word searches and would function in such cases to 'repair' (in the ex-

tended sense of this term: see Schegloff et al. 1977:
363) the silence occasioned by the search. The speaker
using YKb in a case like (71) or (72) is saying, in effect, "You know what I'm getting at, even if this word/
formulation for the moment escapes me".

Such cases could be dismissed on grounds that some
repairable has been covertly deleted and replaced before
being spoken. There is no evidence for this, however. It
is not enough to cite cases of X-YK-X' repairs as representing the full form of YK repairs, since this assumes,
witout warrant that X-YK-X' is always the full form.

To say that YKb is a hesitation marker is problema-
ical, but only for claiming that it is a marker and not for
the claim that it occurs at points of hesitation. At a
great many repair sites in which YKb occurs it is flanked
on one or both sides by pause. Any mid-utterance pause is
a potential place for a YKb since the speaker has faltered
momentarily and is therefore in danger of seeming communicatively incompetent. To use YKb with its usual contribution in such pauses invites the addressee to sanction
the time-out. Whether the YKb is flanked by pauses or not
is of no consequence on this interpretation--the pauses
simply show that time was taken before the utterance could
be resumed.

To summarize the claims in this section: YK at repair sites is YKb. To claim that this YK "patterns differently than the YK which has been characterized as a
discourse particle and move marker" (Goldberg 1980:218)
presupposes, without justification, that there is such a
distinction. YKb has its usual use in positions of hesitation or misstep; with its core use it there invites addressees to go along with the discontinuity on the grounds
that the speaker knows what he or she wants to get across
but temporarily lacks a proper formulation. If the dis-

continuity is too great to go along with (e.g. dog/cat),
a stronger phrase like I mean is apt to be used. YKb implies that the speaker hopes the addressee can divine the
continuation or grasp the point of the unfinished utterance. Use of I mean is more likely when the speaker
thinks the addressee cannot (cf. 6.3 below).

5.8 YKb as a 'Sympathetic Circularity Sequence'

Bernstein (1962a:238) classifies YK as a 'sociocentric
sequence', a term describing the conceptual content of his
term 'sympathetic circularity sequence'. Bernstein has
proposed an elabroate sociological account of the use of
these sequences in conversation.

The 'S.C.' class includes YK and tags such as isn't
it, ain't it, and wouldn't he, all of which are also designated 'terminal sequences'. Bernstein found that S.C.
sequences are used more by working class speakers than by
middle class speakers (1962a:224). His explanation for
this finding is given in terms of the widely-discused distinction between restricted and elaborated codes (Bernstein 1961a, 1961b, 1962a, 1962b), the claim being that
S.C. sequences occur far more in restricted than elaborated codes.

Restricted codes are thought to be less explicit, and
one who uses such a code is thought to assume much about
knowledge shared by speaker and hearer; speech in a restricted code is therefore condensed and less redundant
than speech in an elaborated code (1962a:235).

Bernstein's hypothesis about the sociological function of S.C. sequences is intricate and far-reaching. At
its core, however, are the following observations:

The S.C. sequences may be transmitted as a response of
the speaker to the condensation of his own meanings.

The speaker requires assurance that the message has been received and the listener requires an opportunity to indicate the contrary. It is as if the speaker is saying 'Check--are we together on this?'. On the whole the speaker expects affirmation (1962b:235).

...these sequences may set up different constraints on the flow of communication, particularly on its logical development and elaboration. Inasmuch as the S.C. sequences, which are generated basically by uncertainty, invite implicit affirmation of the previous sequence then they tend to close communication in a particular area rather than facilitate its development and elaboration. The sequences tend to act to maintain the reduction in redundancy and so the condensation of meaning (ibid. 237)

Only highlights of Bernstein's reasoning are presented in these quotations. His interpretation of YK, though limited to final 'tag' position (where a minority of the total instances of YK occur) depend on the item's having a use very near that proposed in 5.5 for YKb. His formulation 'Check--Are we together on this?' is suitably vague with regard to whether the speaker and addressee are in agreement with respect to the <u>truth</u> of the proposition tagged by YK. In the data for the present study cases frequently occur where YKb accompanies a proposition the truth of which the addressee is in no position to ascertain:

   (73)   ... Yesterday I was in my bedroom, YK? And the air conditioning doesn't even cool it off ... LAB-B,10)

   (74)   EVA: =You didn't see that postcard, it's a-=
                               [
          SUE: uh-uh.
          EVA: =Huh! It's a shopping cart? Full of pot,
                                    [
          SUE: (Mm)
          SUE: ((Laughs))
          EVA: Pot all over on the ground, too, YK?
               (LAB-A,8]

   (75)   ... I had a friend who took it an(d) she said it was a piece o(f) cake. She got an 'A' out o(f) the course YK an(d) no trouble really ... (LAB-B 8]

(76)   ... there's this sheriff ... He hit a person- uh
        (th)at was in jail with a ball bat an(d) every-
        thing YK ... (LAB-A)

Bernstein's implication that terminal YK occurs at
points where the speaker's meaning has been condensed is
consistent with the core use proposed above in 5.5, but at
odds with the TT proposal. It should be possible to statistically examine the consequences of Bernstein's claim.
What would be needed would be an objective measure of condensation of meaning. Lacking this, Bernstein's claim,
though elegant, remains undemonstrated.

The range of uses of final YK is much wider than
that discussed by Bernstein. This range should include
locutions that are problematic for the rarity, slanginess,
etc. of the words in them:

(77)   God, (he) went to all this trouble (   ) I'm
        meeked out, YK?   (LAB-A,13)

for difficulties relating to sequential relevance of an
utterance:

(78)   (In this passage SUE tries to prove to EVA that
        FREDDY feels helpless as a shopper and hates to
        shop; the YK tagged utterance does not itself
        show this but sets up a situation in which the
        main point of the talk is then illustrated)

        SUE: He hates the- He went ... shoppin(g) him
        and (h)is brother and (h)is sister went
        Christmas shoppin(g) when (h)e bought me my
        brown pants YK? - and he said- he was just
        like losin(g) it ... (LAB-A,13)

for difficulties having to do with whether the addressee
shares appreciation of some aspect of common experience:

(79)   I was- ... dumb freshman ... comin(g) from
        the hicks. Here I thought I was gonna take
        over the whole world YK? (LAB-A,63).

for the awkwardness of their wording:

- 128 -

> (80)　Big- He thinks he's a big man walkin(g) tall guy
> YK?　(LAB-A,29)

and so on. Whether these different possibilities can all
properly be considered 'condensations' is questionable.
What they do have in common is the fact that they represent discourse situations in which a speaker might wish to
check up on the correspondence of his or her own communicative aims to what the addressee has been able to grasp
from what has been said.

5.9　Interrogative YK

The interrogative use of YK mentioned and exemplified
frequently above is very common, though not predominant,
in the conversational materials used for this study.　For
example, of 74 YKb's in LAB-A 17 are interrogative (23%).
Goldberg (1980:135-6,170) considers this type of YK to be
equivalent in function to declarative TT YK and specifically argues against calling it a turn-exit device (see
5.10 below).　YK? will be treated here as simply the interrogative counterpart of declarative YKb.　The positive
expectation that accompanies the declarative carries over
to the interrogative, but the speaker asks, in effect,
"Isn't this positive expectation of understanding warranted?"

First note that YK? does not serve well as the interrogative counterpart of non-particle YK.　It is difficult
to get a 'literal' (non-particle) reading for YK? in a
sentence like

> (81)　I like oranges, YK?

This sentences would not typically be used as a paraphrase
of:

> (82)　YK that I like oranges?

Rather (81) seems to invite a YKb reading and is thus better paraphrased by:

(83)   I like oranges, you know what I mean?

I find this to be true even with a substantial intonation break between <u>oranges</u> and YK in (81). But the dispreference for a non-YKb reading in sentences like (81) is probably due to the accessibility of the YKb reading, rather than to the unacceptability of the other reading. Thus notice that

(84)   I like oranges, you knew?

in which the YKb reading is not in competition does easily permit a reading in which <u>I like oranges</u> is semantically the complement of <u>you knew</u>.

If YK? has interrogative force, it could be followed by a response of some kind on the part of the addressee. In fact, this is often what happens. The following examples are taken from LAB-A [19,54,58]:

(85)   SUE: ... I was thinkin(g) o(f)- writin(g) a
              check for Jean (a)n(d) Mom's (a)n(d)
              spendin(g) the rest o(f) that whole- my
              whole paycheck on me YK?
       EVA: YEAH.

(86)   EVA: I mean when- when (h)e's not drunk he won't
              talk t(o) me - as though I didn't even
              exist YK?
       SUE: Yeah. - He's too shy ta talk t(o) you...

(87)   SUE: ... But ya see three i(t)'d hafta be like
              th(e) whole summer, YK?
                    (p)
       EVA: Yeah.

(88)   SUE: ... that's all I can see is - like eighty
              million buildings a(h)ll (th)e way around
              me YK?   (   )
                        [
       EVA: Really

In cases where no verbal response occurs, there may have been a nonverbal one; or, since the question rou-

tinely expects a positive response, silence may be taken
as compliance.

In the RTS transcript callers to a radio talk show
frequently use YKb, but in 169 instances, there is not a
single case of interrogative YK. A possible reason for
this is that callers realized that in conversations with a
talk show host--with anonymous listeners potentially num-
bering in the thousands--it was not fully appropriate to
ask for confirmation of understanding, the host being the
only person in a position to respond.

5.10   YK and Turn Taking

Several writers have proposed a connection between YK
and the turn-taking system for conversation.

1. _Utterance lengthener_. Jefferson (1973:69ff) has
characterized YK as an 'utterance lengthener and has
referred to it as a 'standard completion signal' (1972:
329). As a lengthener, YK is classed with other items,
such as _an' everything_, "which indicate to the recipient
that the utterance can have been completed so that he may
begin to talk, while as well providing that the ongoing
speaker has not stopped talking" (1973:69). The function
of YK in this view depends on its placement at a point of
possible utterance termination. YK in itself is only a
signal that "can be included among a series of utterables
which provide that a speaker has not stopped talking
although a possible utterance has been produced" (1973:
73). Tag-positioned address terms, when also used this
way, are described as "mere sound" and as "sound parti-
cle(s) in the service of another type of interactional
work" (1973:74).

Utterance lengtheners may be used after what Jefferson calls a "problematic component", as in (89):

```
(89)  Jim:    And a goodlooking girl comes up to you
              asks you y'know,
      Roger:  Gi(hh)rl asks you to- Alright
```

The lengthener here indicates "that one does not intend to talk about" the problematic component, "by REPLACING such talk with a signal that transition is now underway" (1973: 69).

Note that Jefferson is here talking about YK as an item that can occur after a problematic component, but this is not considered an essential feature of its use as a lengthener. She finds that it is in general a 'standard completion signal' which displays the speaker's willingness for the recipient to begin talking during or right after the signal, but, because it allows the present speaker to continue talking, does not make the more pointed offer of turn that would be made if the present holder of the turn simply stopped talking and waited for another to begin.

Jefferson refers to YK? as a 'plea' (1973:74) which is, like the declarative, an utterance lengthener, though presumably the status of YK? as a plea would preclude its being considered a meaningless particle of sound.

2. <u>Sociocentric sequence</u>. Duncan and Fiske (1977) consider YK to be a 'sociocentric sequence' (see 5.8 above), listing as other examples of this class <u>but uh</u> and <u>or something</u>. Such items (<u>like</u> is excluded; ibid. 170), are described as being "stereotyped expressions" which typically follow "a more substantive statement" (171).

They regard sociocentric sequences as one type of 'speaker turn signal' (185) indicating the speaker's willingness to yield the turn. As such, sociocentric sequences are one of several kinds of turn signals, the others being: occurrence of an intonation marked phonemic clause; completion of a grammatical clause; 'paralinguistic drawl'; onset of gestural signals; and "decrease of paralinguistic pitch and/or loudness on a sociocentric sequence" either during the whole sequence, or its final syllable(s).

Duncan and Fiske thus agree with Sacks et al that YK is 'transition relevant'--inviting a change of speaker turn. This raises the question of how often the turn offer embodied in the use of YK is actually accepted by auditors. If turn changes occur frequently, this would support the claim that YK is a turn signal. Only a partial and indirect answer to this question is provided in Duncan and Fiske 1977. The answer is indirect because they do not report results for YK alone, but for the entire class of sociocentric sequences. It is partial because the data are grouped in a way that happens to obscure the location of turn attempts with respect to sociocentric sequences: turn attempts <u>during</u> these sequences are tallied, but those occurring just after a sociocentric sequence are lumped together with turn attempts after units not terminating with a sociocentric sequence. We can therefore only look at turn attempts during sociocentric sequences in general. Of 100 attempts in the Duncan and Fiske exploratory study, six occurred in this position. There were, however, 21 back channel responses in this position (i.e. brief responses, e.g. <u>m-hm</u>, offered by an auditor during the turn of another speaker and not used to take the floor). Even the figure of 6/100 is difficult to interpret with respect to the present question since included were turn attempts and back channel responses beginning simultaneously with or even just prior to the onset of the sociocentric sequence. In such cases the turn attempt or back channel response could not be viewed as a response to the sociocentric sequence.

3. <u>Recompleter</u>. Utterance-final YK, according to Sacks et al. (1974:718) is a

generally available 'exit technique' for a turn. That
is, a current speaker having constructed a turn's talk
to a possible transition-relevance space without having
selected a next, and finding no other self-selecting to
be next may, employing his option to continue, do a tag
question, selecting another as next speaker upon the
tag question's completion, and thereby exiting from the
turn. In this regard, the tag question is one member
of a class we may call 'recompleters' ...

Goldberg (1980) criticizes the position of Sacks et
al. on several grounds hoping to establish that terminal
YK is not in fact involved in the dynamics of turn taking,
but is instead better characterized by the TT proposal.
The TT analysis has been argued against in 5.7.2 above,
but Goldberg's arguments against regarding YK as a turn
exit device can be examined on their merits. She suggests
five such arguments.

1. Goldberg claims that the turn exit idea predicts,
falsely, that there should be a pause just prior to YK at
transitional relevance places. The pause is thought necessary for the speaker to ascertain that there are no
self-appointed next speakers (Goldberg 1980:136). The
argument is valid against the specific proposal of Sacks
et al. quoted above, since they require the speaker to
check first to see if self-selection occurs, but YK could
still be a turn exit device without this checking. Moreover, it is not clear on what evidence Goldberg bases the
claim that pauses to check for self-selection do not occur.

2. Goldberg argues that there are cases of turns interrupted during items following issue of a YK at a transition relevance point (1980:136). This alone is not a
valid argument against the turn exit idea since it presupposes that the interrupting speaker wished to interrupt
earlier, at the point just following YK, and did not. The
decision to interrupt could, however, be made at or just
before the point of interruption itself.

- 134 -

3. Goldberg argues that the turn exit idea is faulty because there are cases of locution-final YK that are turn-medial.[11] These, however, cannot be used to argue against YK as a turn exit device, since it is presupposed that all turn offers are accepted, which is certainly not to be expected (see Sacks et al. 1974:706).

4. Goldberg cites the following instance of overlapped YK:

```
(90)   Ken:     She's gotta gun in it.  She's gotta gun
                hangin' there?  And I said what's the gun
                for.  She said in case any a' my neigh-
                bors wanna come in, // yuh know?
       Al:      heh
       Roger:   hehh.  An' she invi(h)tes you i(h)n to//
                see it.   hehh
       Ken:     Y/know?
       Ken:     I s'd- well // well you know, all yer
                neighbors've gotta do is just put a lit-
                tle mud in that little air hole up there
                in the top an' yer all done.  eheh.
                [GTS:2:2:19]   (Goldberg 1980:137)
```

She argues that "on the basis of Ken's immediately subsequent 'turn' it appears that Ken has not, in fact, completed his turn which ended with Al's and Roger's interruptions. Ken demonstrates the unwarranted nature of the interruption by his interruption of Roger" (Goldberg: 1980:137). This example could, however, equally well be taken as evidence that YK is a turn exit device, since Roger takes it as the occasion to begin a turn of his own.

5. Similarly, Goldberg (1981a) argues that turn exiting is irrelevant in cases where the speaker is engaged, for example, in a long narrative and obviously wants to retain the floor until completion of the narrative. A problem with this argument is that in Goldberg's examples none of the YK's are interrogative, and it is specifically interrogative YK's that Sacks et al. claim

are instances of turn exiting (see the quotation at the beginning of this section). This argument thus falls beside its target.

The position taken in the present work is that neither Goldberg's TT account nor the Sacks et al. view of YK? as a turn exit device is adequate. Terminal YK? only once immediately precedes a turn change in the LAB data, although it does frequently elicit a back channel response, such as m-hm, uh-huh, or yeah (12 back channel responses to 24 instances of YK?). This is what would be expected if YK? were to make its usual YKb contribution. We would not expect a full change of turn, but simply a brief response to the speaker's question (i.e. to, roughly, "You follow, don't you?") or a perfunctory nod of agreement, or at the very least a cooperative silence. This position is in harmony with Goldberg in claiming that the turn exit idea is incorrect. But the YK's in question cannot be assigned TT status by default.

5.11 Distribution of YK: Some Quantitative Results

In this section the occurrence of tokens of YKb in the LAB and RTS materials is examined quantitatively.

1. YK and filled pause. In popular works on language use, and even in more scholarly research, the idea recurs that YK is a hesitation form amounting to nothing more than a filled pause. This view is, of course, squarely at odds with the claim that YKb has a specifiable use and that it is this use that determines where YKb is used in conversation. The present treatment therefore predicts that there will be differences between the positions of occurrence of YKb and those of filled pause. Such predictions are easily tested, since both filled pauses (um, uh) and YKb occur in large numbers in the tapes used for this study.

Uh (cf. Ch. 2 and 6) may be viewed as an evincive item indicating that the speaker's thoughts are momentarily null, unclear, or unpresentable. As such, uh issued mid-utterance expresses that the speaker has faltered for some reason but hopes to be able to continue.[12] If the uh is followed by silence, a problem arises: the speaker may be seen as wishing to continue but unable to do so. This both constitutes a face threat to the speaker, whose conversational competence or cooperativeness might be doubted, and can lead to unwanted loss of the turn.

Mid-utterance YK, on the other hand, is a sign not that the speaker is simply faltering, but that the speaker is actively and competently engaged in the communication. This follows from the core use of YKb to indicate that the speaker is concerned with whether what is said is 'getting across', recognizes that there may be some difficulty on the addressee's part in this regard, and displays current control of his or her communicative role as turn-holder by acknowledging this difficulty before continuing. YKb, because it demonstrates control, is especially apt to occur in situations where an addressee might suspect that this control has been lost. Since the position in which uh has just been issued is one such place, we might expect YKb to commonly follow uh and there to serve as an attempt to reassert control.

The tapes were examined for cases of adjacent uh and YKb to see whether these items appear significantly more often in the order uh YK than the other way around. YKb occurs adjacent to uh frequently in the RTS transcripts, but only once in the face-to-face conversations. This may reflect the relative casualness/formality of these two speaking situations. The face-to-face conversations are more fluent and relaxed than the RTS conversations, no doubt because the latter took place before a vast and imaginably astute radio audience. In situations of moderate casualness (e.g. the Pear Story recountings, Chafe 1980), a moderate number of YK and _uh_ adjacencies are found.

In the RTS material 45 cases of adjacent YKb and _uh_ occur. Of these 35 are in the order _uh_ YK, and ten are in the opposite order (chi-square 6.94; p<.01; df=1).

Unfilled pauses are an even more stark sign of loss of control; relatively more pauses before than after YKb would therefore be expected. This expectation is strongly confirmed by the present data. Of 117 adjacencies of YK and pause, 88 are with the pause preceding, 19 with it following (chi-square 14.88; p<.001; df=1).

Two other differences in the way YKb and _uh_ pattern were noted: i) In many cases some item is followed by YKb after which that item is exactly repeated before the speaker continues. These are clause-internal 'restarts', as in

(91)   ... they can get- YK they can get close (ta you)
        [RTS18,56]
(92)   ... for instance they YK they have a- an area
        where ...   [RTS6,52]

YK is significantly less likely to intermit in these cases than is _uh_ (ratio clause internal restarts with YK to all clause-internal YK's = 1/46; for _uh_ = 15/76; chi-square 16.68; p<.001; df=1). Why this should be the case is not clear; ii) The proposed core use of YKb provides an explanation for the tendency of _uh_ to occur much more frequently than YK after conjunctions. In issuing a conjunction, the speaker gives the addressee little to go on for the purpose of guessing what might come next. Conjunctions can be used to hold the speaking turn before the speaker has planned anything substantive to say. We would therefore expect to find _uh_ after conjunctions more fre-

- 138 -

quently than YK, and this is the case[13] (YK after con-
junctions/total YK's = 23/347; for _uh_ = 114/459; chi-
square 46.44; p<.001; df=1).

5.12 Conclusion

In this chapter various hypotheses about the function
of the discourse particle YK were examined. In each case
it was argued that some particular function can be served
by YKb because the basic use of the item is appropriate to
that function. As in previous chapters, the intent was
not to show that the item does not have multiple functions, but to show that a unified account of these functions proceeds naturally from considering how the basic
use of the item is interpretable in particular conversational contexts. It is therefore inaccurate to consider
YKb to be a 'device' especially 'marking' these functions.
This claim would be odd in the same way that it would be
odd, for example, to claim that "Brrr" is a device for
getting someone to close the window. Certainly this is
one function this item can serve, but if it is considered
a marker, we face the uncomfortable prospect of an essentially infinite set of such markers and of marked functions.

These remarks should be tempered with some discussion
of the conventionalization or routinization of YKb. It
is certainly true that, as a standard way of seeking or
inviting confirmation of understanding, YKb has come to be
routinely associated with several common conversational
situations in which the speaker is uncertain of how well
s/he is getting across. But the routinization has not
obliterated the core use of YKb, since, as in the case of
well and _like_, the core use is consistent with the routine
functions. In this chapter statistical evidence was
brought to bear on this issue: distributional tendencies

of the item demonstrate the relevance of the core use of YKb to its placement in conversation.

This analysis complements earlier functional analyses of YK by providing an answer to a fundamental question these other analyses raise: Why is the particular item YKb used for the specific functions it is, rather than some other item?

The basic use of YKb proposed above is not in the nature of a discovery--many writers have tried to specify the use of the item, and some have come relatively close to the formulation used in the present work. The addition attempted here has been to refine the statement of the core use of YKb by relating it to disclosure and to demonstrate the connection between the core use and the diverse functional claims that have been made about YK.

YKb is not associated with certain discourse functions because it 'marks' them (a very strong claim) but because its basic use is appropriate to each such function. Earlier effort to identify distinct functions of YKb was not, however, wasted: we must understand both the individual functions and their underlying unity to have a balanced and complete account of this particle. Note, though, that rather than claiming that the discourse structural properties of YKb are basic, the present study claims that the context-free value of the item underlies its specific functions in discourse.

The great frequency of occurrence of YKb in conversation is predictable from its core use. It appears in so many different places because this use is appropriate at any point at which the speaker is unsure of how well s/he is coming across. YKb is at home--though clearly optional--wherever the speaker feels that what s/he has just said or will just now say in the shared world may not have its desired effect in the other world. The frequency of

use of YKb would be expected to differ depending on many
factors, including the relationship between conversants
(e.g., whether 'superiors' speaking to 'inferiors' deem it
appropriate to predict confirmation of understanding), the
degree of fluency they experience in particular conversational situations, their feelings about their own use or
overuse of YK, and what they perceive to be the importance
of addressee understanding of their intentions.

CHAPTER SIX

THE ROLE OF DISCOURSE PARTICLES IN CONVERSATION

6.1 General Remarks

This study has focused attention on the discourse particles _like_, _well_, and _you know_, attempting to isolate a single core use for each one. This was possible in each case: _like_ indicates a possible minor nonequivalence of what the current speaker will now immediately say (or has just now said) and what the speaker now has (or just now had) in mind to convey; _well_ indicates that the speaker, at the time _well_ is uttered, is consulting his or her current thoughts; _you know_ (YKb) checks (with a positive expectation) on the correspondence between what the speaker intends to convey and what the addressee can grasp in regard to what the speaker has just said or is about to say. In each case this core use survives regardless of the 'local' reason the speaker may have for using the item at a particular position in discourse; and in each case the set of functions the item may serve makes sense in terms of its core use. Previous analyses of these items have not attended closely to the question of whether such a core use can be formulated, so that although various functions for each particle have been identified, these analyses are in general unable to explain why individual particles serve the specific functions they do.

The question of what the linguistic contribution of these items is is complicated by their routinization as standard ways of dealing with recurrent conversational situations. Thus, for example, _well_ can be used as a conventional way to introduce an abrupt change of topic. The point repeatedly made above regarding the varied con-

- 141 -

versational uses of these items is that the items do not, simply by virtue of becoming routines, lose their basic use. This is indicated by the fact that the routine conversational uses of each item are consistent with its basic use, and by the fact that when the particles are scrutinized in situ in discourse their basic use illuminates descriptions offered by subjects of the 'meaning' of utterances containing the items (see 3.5).

Probably the failure of subjects to be able to isolate immediately the core use of like, well, and YKb is largely due to their inability to differentiate between the core use and contextual or pragmatic factors, an expected and very general limitation on the usefulness of linguistic intuitions.

In the most general portrayal these particles are all related to the disclosure of covert thinking. They all represent responses to problems arising due to the 'invisibility' of undisclosed thinking. Each participant in a conversation is aware of three spheres of conversation-related activity: the private world of current disclosable thought; the shared world in which speakers collaborate in placing in view linguistic, paralinguistic, and kinesic elements in a particular sequence; and the other world, containing disclosable but otherwise unapparent thinking of some co-participant(s).

The particles like and well (and many others: see Ch. 2) are evincives: they permit the speaker to bring up, without thereby specifying, contents of the private world. Such items are a means of calling attention in a general way to the relevance at some particular point in discourse of thinking the speaker leaves partially undisclosed. The reasons for such partial disclosure are varied, depending on context and the speaker's communicative abilities and intentions. Notice that while ordinary lexical items may be spoken accompanied by undisclosed thinking, only evincives specifically indicate that some such undisclosed thinking is under way.

YKb responds to the disclosure problem in a different way: here the speaker is concerned about the undisclosed contents of the other world and is, in particular, interested in whether the desired effect of his or her words obtains in that other world. A positive response or a peaceable silence is anticipated, indicating that the private and other worlds are thought, in essential respects, to be in harmony.[1]

A distinction should be drawn between the disclosure just discussed and the kind solicited when asking a question such as, "What time is it?" By using this sentence the speaker seeks disclosure of information, but not specifically of thinking then current in the addressee's mind. The concept of disclosure relevant in the case of the discourse items well, like, and YKb is of current (in real time) thought arising in connection with the events of an ongoing conversation.[2] Each of these items thus inhabits or responds to the now of actual talk rather than some imagined, recalled, or projected now. The frequent characterization of these items as lubricants, punctuation devices, and so on, hints at their temporally local domain. Even when retrospectively quoted, such particles occupy some real (albeit reported) now at which they were spoken (cf. Ch. 2). They represent an acknowledgment by speakers that, despite the negotiated pace of actual talk, in both the private and the other worlds thinking runs apace: covert reactions occur at some sequentially present moment and must be placed, or at least evinced, in the shared world if they are to be jointly known about and responded to.

Previous work on conversational behavior has largely and understandably been limited to what occurs in the
shared world. As repeatedly and correctly stated by sociologists, what occurs there can be understood in terms of
what else is said and done what stands 'bones out' for
examination. The logic of the shared world of talk and
other behavior is accessible because in general speakers
place in that world what they mean to be understandable.
On the other hand, however inaccessible they are to the
nonparticipant researcher, the private and other worlds
are of no less importance to the <u>participants</u> in a conversation than is the shared one. In fact, a major question
for the speaker in conversation is how to effectively introduce what is private into the shared world, and how to
properly and effectively obtain disclosure from the other
world. A useful analogy is a poker game.

If we limit our attention to the shared world of
talk, we thereby exclude two 'thirds' of what is involved
when people converse. The importance of the unseen aspects of conversation is shown by the very frequent use in
conversation of discourse particles that specifically relate the covert worlds to the overt one. What conversants
are thinking to themselves, unless disclosed or inferable
from what is said or done by them, perforce remains a mys-
tery to anyone but them, but we can watch conversants
orient in their talk to what is undisclosed and perform an
and solicit partial disclosures, and we can be mindful of
the fact that linguistic behavior, from the speaker's van-
tage point, is even richer and more complex than displayed, recordable speech. This is not only a matter of
some things being 'between the lines'--a problem of inferences and implicatures--but of material that underlies the
proceedings but is not knowable by all the co-conversants.

- 145 -

The following several sections will provide a more general perspective on the discourse particles found in English conversation by asking what kinds of disclosure functions these particles serve, using for this purpose work by others on particles beyond the three already treated at length above. (Some of these additional particles are first mentioned in Ch. 2.)

6.2 Now

Schiffrin (1981b) finds that the 'discourse marker' now is used "to preface evidence, to precede a change in topic or sub-topic, a switch from main to subordinate topic, a switch in speaker stance, in speaker-hearer relationship, and so on" (14), and abstracts two common features of these environments: "they open something new and current in the discourse context (and there is) some kind of switch, or contrast with the immediately adjacent discourse" (14-15).

This analysis of now fits the data of the present study, but a slightly different characterization of the use of now will be offered here based on the notion of disclosure. In this connection it is of interest that now opens "something new and current". In this respect now is aligned with well, like, and YKb in being tied to a particular discourse moment.[3] We do not find the particle now leaving the present speaker's moment of utterance, though the adverb may of course do so:

(1) They saw that they were now in the deepest part of the jungle.

Items tied to their moment of utterance may be viewed as intrusions from the private world. Lakoff (1974) suggests the word 'stance' for what such items indicate. This may be clarified: it is the speaker's current stance

- 146 -

toward what is right now occurring or has just now occurred or will now immediately occur in the conversation. The time line of the shared world is dictated by requirements of turn taking, topic development, sequencing conventions, discourse strategies, and the necessity of taking time to 'say out' what may have already come to mind. The items being discussed here, however, although placed at particular points on the collaborative time line, are used and taken as current reflections of the private world.

Viewed this way, now is an item by which a speaker indicates that s/he views what s/he will now be saying[4] as in some unspecified way a 'switch' from what has come just before and, by contrasting what came before with what is said next, also represents a larger continuity subsuming the switch. Thus now at the beginning of a lecture or a meeting, evokes some pre-existing situation which (within the confines of the entire proceeding) will now be abandoned in favor of an ensuing one. Now is an evincive since it has the two coincident properties of evincives: it is tied to the speaker's now of actual utterance[5], and it indicates but does not specify current covert thinking on the part of the speaker. The second property is reflected in the fact that now indicates some discontinuity-within-continuity perceived by the speaker but left to the addressee to (if possible) determine the precise nature of.[6] The speaker is saying in effect, "This belongs here, but my reasons for saying so remain to be brought up later in the shared world, or left for you (the addressee) to infer, guess at, ignore, or inquire about." Like well, when that particle is used as a topic introducer (see 4.4), now provides that the switch is one that is undertaken knowingly.

6.3 I mean

The discourse item I mean is discussed at length in Goldberg (1976, 1980); Crystal and Davy (1975) devote two concise pages to it. As suggested by a literal reading, the item is useful in repair situations where it "marks the contribution as a modifying or clarifying continuation of the previous (usually the speaker's own) contribution" (Goldberg 1980:124-5). The functions of the item in particular discourse environments may vary according to how the basic corrective or clarifying core use is applicable in the particular context at hand. Thus I mean "may redirect the ongoing talk by introducing 'modifications' which both correct and add to to previous contribution" (125), or it may regain the floor (251a) by signaling "that the intervening turn interrupted the speaker" (127), or, in utterance medial position, "tends to repair a prior phonological or grammatical error" (244). The description of the item offered by Crystal and Davy is essentially in harmony with Goldberg's. They claim

> The meaning of this phrase is extraordinarily difficult to define: it seems to perform a variety of semantic functions, some of which are more important than others in any given instance. Generally speaking, its main function is to indicate that the speaker wishes to clarify the meaning of his immediately preceding expression. This clarification may stem from a number of reasons and take a number of forms (1975:97).

In the framework of the present study, I mean can be regarded as an item with a disclosure function. I mean is used to indicate that what the speaker has said and what the speaker has in mind to express are not well matched. Or one might say that I mean indicates a nonequivalence of what is in the shared world and what is in the private world. This is similar to the characterization of like, but the items differ in that like indicates a minor non-

- 148 -

equivalence, one the speaker finds unlikely to result in an important misunderstanding of the intended meaning, while I mean indicates that what is said and what is meant may well be substantially nonequivalent and, unless repair is undertaken, could lead to misunderstanding. It is thus important that I mean, but not like, prefaces corrections.

I mean is evincive since it is tied to its moment of utterance and indicates but does not itself specify the nature of the nonequivalence the speaker finds to exist between what is said and what is meant. Typically the speaker's intention is spelled out in what follows I mean,[7] but I mean is often used utterance-terminally with intonation suggesting a continuation that is never supplied but which addressees are presumed capable of intuiting.

6.4 Mind you

Mind you as a feature of British English is discussed in Crystal and Davy (1975:99-100). They comment:

> This is another phrase whose meaning is extremely difficult to delimit. We have noted a number of different 'strands' of meaning, of which the most important seems to be the expression of some kind of contradiction, with a reduced or apologetic force. The speaker feels the need to state a different or additional viewpoint from what he or other speakers have already expressed, but he wishes to do this without causing offense ... In addition, mind you is used to express the speaker's awareness that he is (a) saying something controversial, and is worried about the possibility of being disagreed with later, or (b) saying something which he thinks is obvious but which his listener may dispute (100).

Taking this description at face value, it would seem that the use of mind you resembles that of other particles so far discussed, but that the specific function of this item is to indicate a nonequivalence of what the speaker has injected into the shared world and what s/he expects may have arisen or may just now arise in the other world as a result. The item is thus also characterizable as having a disclosure function in that it indicates the possibility of the topical relevance but ultimate insignificance, incorrectness, etc. of what has just arisen or may well presently arise in the other world.

6.5 Sort o(f), Kind o(f); An(d) stuff, An(d) everything, An(d) so on, etc.

Such items as sort o(f) and kind o(f) (discussed in Crystal and Davy 1975:98-9) were claimed above (3.7) to be related in function to like in indicating a possible minor nonequivalence of what is said and what is meant. The Crystal and Davy description accords with this assessment: "These phrases may be used immediately before any word or phrase about which there is uncertainty, vagueness, or idiosyncracy". Such phrases may also follow the item in question, of course:

(2) She was carrying it in her hands sort of.

Such items differ from like in that they cannot be used initially:

(3) *Sort of, I handed her my letter of intent.

Another set of items can be used utterance-finally to indicate that the speaker is not saying everything that might be said. For example:

(4) He came home last night bangin(g) the door an(d) everything. (Lab-A,30)
(5) Somebody would have to get up at four o'clock in the morning to take me to Wooster y'know and all that stuff. (LAB-A,36)
(6) I really don't think they'd play in any bar or anything (LAB-A,22)

These latter items fairly obviously indicate that some

contents of the private world are being withheld from the shared world because they would add nothing essential to what has been said, or because for some other reason the speaker chooses not to express them. They therefore evince the availability of more material in the private world than is presented in the shared world.

6.6 Interjections

There appears to be a fundamental identity between many of the items traditionally referred to as interjections and those considered discourse particles or markers. Many interjections represent partial intrusions from the private world and respond to the problem of disclosure. Some of these items, because of their basic use, have multiple discourse functions connected with such notions as topic development and topic change, but all share the property of being free, in interpretation if not always in placement, of the 'negotiated' time line of shared talk, and they acknowledge the existence, relevance, and (most often) general tenor of undisclosed thought. The use of several items first discussed in Chapter 2 can now be more fully appreciated:

1. Oh_1 indicates that the speaker has just now become aware of something and wishes to display that this private world event, the exact nature of which is not specified by oh_1, has occurred.

2. Oh_2 indicates that the speaker has now paused to make a decision or choice between alternatives, no one of which is the correct or accurate one (see James 1974:84); the item is evincive because the alternatives and the course of the decision process are not displayed by oh_2 itself.

3. Oh_3 is similar in use to well; it evinces introspection.

4. Hey indicates that the speaker is with thought at the time of uttering hey and desires the addressee's attention in order to place material into the shared world. (Note that hey is also commonly self-addressed--with odd effect.)

5. Aha indicates that the speaker has just now covertly pieced together the logic of a situation or seen a connection previously missed. The particulars of the connection seen are not displayed by using aha itself.

6. Ah indicates that the speaker has just now thought of something and finds that thing, or having thought of it, pleasing or significant (see James 1974: 37), but does not itself indicate what the thing is.

7. Uh, according to James (1974:87), indicates that the "speaker is hesitating to try to think of the best or most accurate thing to say next, or to remember something, or is reluctant to say what is to follow". She adds, "uh is very commonly used when the speaker has any uncertainty at all about what he is saying, or about whether he is using the right words, or even about how his addressees are reacting to him." The use she assigns to uh is thus not very specific. Apparently uh is used when the speaker has paused for any reason at all and wishes to mark this as a point of pause, rather than as a definitive halt. James shows that there are several differences between uh and the other interjections she studied, but looking at her arguments carefully, one finds that in every case the 'meaning difference' is a result of some other interjection having an element of meaning that uh lacks. Uh thus appears to mark pauses of unspecified nature.

In every case the interjections listed above are capable of serving as discourse particles in the sense that

with their basic contribution they can take on particular
discourse functions. Even uh can assume such a function
if uttered in the proper context. Consider the possible
discourse repercussions of an uh audibly spoken by a member of the audience three sentences into a formal lecture.

6.7   Types of Disclosure Functions

Table 4 summarizes and groups the disclosure functions of particles considered in this study. This is not
a complete listing of English discourse particles, but
does include the items found in quantity in the present
data. Individual items listed within each category in
Table 4 have contrasting functions in most cases but fall
within the general disclosure function given to the right.
Most of the functions displayed in Table 4 involve relationships between the private world and the shared world.
This is what would be anticipated, since the other world
is, by definition, inaccessible to the speaker. The particles that do function with respect to the other world
either question or speculate about what the addressee is
thinking. One would not expect to find particles the primary function of which is, for example, to indicate that
something has suddenly arisen in the other world. To
claim the existence of undisclosed thought in the other
world is an act ripe with potentially disruptive implications ('you are predictable--your mind is an open book').

The taxonomy in Table 4 raises several questions
which fall beyond the scope of the present invesitgation
but which require answers before discourse particle
function can be fully elucidated. A major question is
whether languages differ significantly in the types of disclosure functions served by their discourse particles. The
same question may be asked about dialects and individuals'

TABLE 4

DISCLOSURE FUNCTIONS OF SOME DISCOURSE PARTICLES

(P=Private world, S=Shared world, O=Other world)

Particle	Indicates
well	thought in progress in P
let me see	"
oh_3	"
aha	thought has suddenly arisen in in P
ah	"
oh_1	"
man	"
hey	"
uh	thought temporarily not in progress in P
um	"
like	$P \cong S$
sort o(f)	"
kind o(f)	"
I mean	$P \neq S$
an(d) everything	$P < S$
an(d) stuff	"
oh_2	"
y(ou) know (YKb)	$P \stackrel{?}{=} O$
mind you	$P \neq O$

conversational styles. Are some discourse particle functions found universally, or are particles with functions that are forseeable and potentially useful rare or entirely missing? Answers to such questions should indicate something about the dynamics of conversational behavior. It is hoped that the taxonomy presented in Table 4, though limited to English, will suggest lines of comparative research on disclosure phenomena which will provide a clearer idea of how speakers relate public to private when they speak.

6.8 General Summary

The problem of disclosure arises within the general communicative purpose of speech because conversants are engaged in a complex form of behavior in which some of what occurs in displayed, while thoughts may remain undisclosed. Speakers frequently call attention, for reasons varying with their communicative aims, to what is occurring beneath the 'visible' surface of a conversation. The disclosure problem is that what is covert may to some extent and for some reason be communicatively relevant to what is said and done. In this study the function of items usually called discourse particles and interjections has been examined. It was found that each such item has a core use related to disclosure and, based on that use, a variety of secondary functions depending on specific conversational contexts.

Each of the items discussed is used, generally speaking, to relate what is covert to what is overt in ongoing conversational activity. The relationships involved here have been described in terms of three 'worlds': the one known to the speaker alone, that known to the addressee(s)[8] alone, and the world known to both. The disclosure problem may in individual cases involve the incongruity be-

tween what is shared and what is private, the invisibility
of the other world to the speaker, the incongruity between
what is presumed to be in the other world and what is in
the private one, and so on.

The particles discussed in this study differ in the
ways in which they respond to the general problem of disclosure. Like is a response to the nonequivalence of what
is shared and what is privately intended; well indicates
in the shared world that consideration is occurring in the
private world; YKb responds to the need of speakers to be
assured of the equivalence of the private and other worlds
(in some crucial respects) with regard to what is being
said. Several other discourse items may be characterized
in similar ways, and it may in fact be true that disclosure
is relevant to the discription of most discourse particles
used in English, including many of the items traditionally
referred to as interjections.

The emphasis here has not been on identifying multiple discourse functions for each particle, but on providing an explanation for why each particle is capable of
serving the functions that it does. In that sense the
view proposed here is not an alternative to multi-func-
tional analyses, but illuminates what is correct in these
other studies both by clarifying the core uses of particular items and providing a general framework in which
their core uses can be compared.

The results of this study also bear on a basic issue
in semantics: that of ambiguity versus vagueness (see
Zwicky and Sadock 1973). For each of the three discourse
particles examined at length above, it has been possible
to find a way through the multiple readings to a single
basic use. Additional readings of each item can be pre-
dicted from features of context and discourse placement.
This work is thus aligned with recent work (e.g. Atlas

1977, Kempson 1980, 1981) suggesting that in most cases it is possible to regard additional understandings of an item as due to lack of specificity rather than to true ambiguity.

Finally, this study indicates that conversation studies must be responsive to a broader range of phenomena than is usually envisioned. So long as conversation is viewed solely as a matter of what is displayed and openly reacted to by conversants and of what is inferable from their behavior, it remains accessible to research. As a working assumption, most conversation studies take the shared world to be somehow independent of what occurs privately in the minds of the conversants. This methodological tack is not only convenient but is recommended by a powerful argument: individual conversants, in choosing what to do and say next, are attentive to what they and their co-conversants have already said and done. Examination of discourse particles such as <u>well</u>, <u>like</u>, and <u>you know</u>, however, points up the fact that individual participants in a conversation are also attentive to the selectivity of disclosure. Therefore, although the private and other worlds are not directly accessible to the nonparticipant observer, their existence cannot be ignored. Discourse particles abound in conversation precisely because by using them speakers can display ongoing sensitivity to the importance of what is not expressed in an interaction.

FOOTNOTES

Chapter 1

[1]This term is apparently due to Goffman. In his words:

> We owe to any social situation in which we find our-
> selves, evidence that we are reasonably alive to what
> is already in it--and furthermore to what may arise,
> whether on schedule or unexpectedly. If need for imme-
> diate action is required of us, we will be ready--if
> not mobilized, mobilizable ... If addressed by anyone
> in the situation, we should not have far to go to re-
> spond (1978:791)

[2]Such prefixes only incidentally tell us that thought
occurred during speech. Their primary use is to usher
in material no longer obviously relevant to what has just
occurred in the conversation. As such they are provisions
for violating the convention that what one says ought
to be discernibly or inferably relatable to what precedes
in the conversation (cf. Grice's Maxim of Relevance).

[3]Deborah Tannen (1979) has experimented with playing back
tapes of conversations in the presence of those who parti-
cipated in them and asking them to explain their contributions. The principal limitation of this invesitagative
tool is obvious: there is no reliable way to check the
accuracy of hindsight. One might also expect subjects
to make subtle (or not so subtle) adjustments when reporting aspects of their intentions which, in retrospect,
they might find unappetizing.

[4]There is an interesting resemblance between the framework
proposed here for the study of discourse particles and
that in Lakoff (1974). For example, the notion that most

- 157 -

sentences "give clues, in one way or another, as to <u>how</u>, precisely, that utterance is to mediate between the speaker's mentality and the real world outside" (p. XVIII-1) is parallel to the claim in the present study that certain linguistic items mediate between the private and the shared worlds. An important difference between these two approaches involves the noncongruity of Lakoff's internal world/real world distinction and the distinction between private and shared worlds in the present work. The private world consists of the current unexpressed thoughts of the speaker in conversation (not the speaker's 'mentality'); and the notion 'shared world' is also relevant to a particular moment in a particular conversation and has nothing directly to do with the notion 'information about the real world' (see Lakoff 1974:XVIII-1).

[5]So phrased, the problem might seem a self-inflicted one, since a speaker can solve the problem, at least insofar as it relates to the private world, by simply disclosing into the shared world what has been left unexpressed. However, as following chapters will make clear, full disclosure is neither the only, nor, interactively speaking, the best approach in every conversational situation; and there is still the matter of other world disclosure, which rests outside the current speaker's direct control.

[6]It does, though, sometimes occur that a speaker carries on two lines of talk in the same conversational 'space'; for example, a speaker may intersperse exchanges with a distant interlocutor with quietly muttered self-addressed remarks.

[7]RTS and LAB examples appearing in this dissertation have been altered to conceal identities. Every attempt has been made not to alter features of examples that are cru-

cial to the analysis. In most cases the alteration has involved only substitution of one proper noun for another.

[8]The seeming casualness of these conversations is not mentioned in support of their suitability as data. The three particles receiving major attention in this study are by no means peculiar to casual speech. If anything, their occurrence is provoked by more formal speaking situations. In the RTS materials, for example, like, well, and y(ou) know occur in large numbers even though callers are presumably aware that what they say may be heard by a large section of the community in which they live.

[9]Reader's transcripts often attempt to indicate correctly the point of onset of overlapping material with respect to what is overlapped, and, sometimes, to indicate the point at which the overlap ends, but only crude attempts, through word spacing, are ever made to indicate what precisely overlaps what during the period of the overlap itself. Transcripts differ widely in how accurately pauses are indicated. Sometimes pauses are recorded to within .1 second; sometimes the pauses are rounded off to the nearest half second or whole second; but often they are not indicated at all. Moreover, reader's transcripts are not usually accompanied by a statement of the degree of their temporal exactness.

Chapter 2

[1]In this study the nominal use of 'evincive' is reserved for particular lexical items with evincive function. One may evince something with novel sentences: I am thinking of a large object with three moving parts. Note, however,

- 160 -

that no single word in the preceding sentence is an evincive, as defined.

[2]Items like _ouch_ are apparently not evincive. They appear
not to serve important routine discourse functions and
are notable for occurring at virtually any point in an
utterance--even within a word. Such items are probably
best described as interruptions (cf. Rotenberg 1978).

[3]Other Gricean maxims may also be involved in specific
cases; for example, "Do not say that for which you lack
adequate evidence" (a clause of the Maxim of Quality)
and "Be brief" (a clause of the Maxim of Manner).

[4]For the purposes of this chapter, turn initiations were
identified using three criteria: i) back channel responses
(e.g. _uh huh_, _my god!_) were not considered to constitute
separate turns; ii) talk intermitted or overlapped by
such back channel responses was considered to constitute
an unbroken turn; iii) only contributions judged to be
clearly substantive following substantive contributions
by a just prior speaker were considered true turn initiations. These criteria are admittedly too conservative.
This limitation seemed necessary, though, in view of the
lack of clear decision procedures for determining the
location of turn changes. Probably any theory of turn
structure would have to admit at least the cases included
for purposes of this statistical count.

[5]This assumption is only relevant for retrospective quotations, but in the present data, and probably in general,
this type of quotation is by far the most common.

[6]Even when speakers quote themselves, the turn changes
in the sense that the self-reported material entails sus-

pension of the presently motivated contributions of talk. The motivation, situational relevance, etc. of the reported material is in some other conversation or situation than the present one.

[7]There are other verbs that enquote, but because their meanings are so specific, their usefulness for enquoting is limited (e.g. print, recite, sing; cf. Sadock 1969:317-319).

[8]The use of pauses, intonational breaks, and the adoption of stylized voice quality are probably of considerable importance in initiating quotations in speech, as well as in unquoting. I would hazard a guess, however, that such cues are not so reliable as one might at first think. I have noticed that the tendency for well to be heard as an initiator is quite strong--so strong that pausing, intonation, and voice quality adjustments cannot 'coax' well out of a quotation. I asked two volunteers to stand before a class and read aloud the following sentences from cards:

    (a) John said, well, "Think of the starving people
         in India.
    (b) Mary said, well, "I like fish".

The volunteers were told to go to whatever lengths neces-sary (in pronouncing the sentences) to make sure that those listening would get the impression that well belonged outside the quotation. Fifteen subjects were asked to write down the sentences just as they heard them, with appropriate punctuation. As the following results show, the subjects were for the most part unable to 'hear' what the two volunteers were saying:

	sentence a	sentence b
<u>well</u> attributed to quoting speaker	4	1
<u>well</u> attributed to quoted speaker	11	14

Chapter 3

[1] Many dictionaries list as dialectal the use of <u>like</u> as a verbal auxiliary meaning 'came near', as in I <u>like to fell out of bed</u>.

[2] This term is due to Lakoff (1972).

[3] This usage is, however, mentioned in an editor's note to Schourup 1982.

[4] In an informal survey of 25 undergraduates at Ohio State University, eight claimed to use the construction regularly and all had heard it. The students all agreed that the quotations it introduces are internal.

[5] 'Thus' is probably an attempt at fluent English translation. It is clear that the item's usual meaning is 'like'.

[6] <u>Webster's Third</u> does list a 'for example' reading for <u>like</u> in its use as a conjunction: <u>when your car gives trouble--like when the motor won't start</u>.

[7] Woolford considers the use of <u>like</u> to be peculiar to California. This is certainly not the case.

[8] Did anyone, except the critics, ever really say "Like Hi!". I suspect that this and other bizarre cases are projections by people who don't approve of nonstandard <u>like</u> and wish to make it seem ludicrous.

[9]The material may precede in the case of sentence final _like_.

[10]Perhaps this should be a query: Do such cases exist?

[11]Wright (1957:637-8) cites a pre-19th century example: _So, like_, I went directly.

[12]Scare quotes are often used in writing to do what _like_ does in its hedge use in speech. Examples are scattered throughout the text of this dissertation.

[13]_Like_ and similar items may also be used for politeness as what House and Kasper (1981) call 'modality markers'. Such hedges can be used to avoid "a precise propositional specification thus circumventing the potential provocation such a specification might entail" (167).

Chapter 4

[1]Goldberg cites Goffman's characterization of conversational moves as having "a distinctive unitary bearing on some set or other of the circumstances in which participants find themselves" (Goffman 1976:272).

[2]Goldberg entertains a fallback position in which rather than marking move type, discourse particles merely _reinforce_ move type (1980:127), a much weaker and vaguer claim.

[3]The reason for this particular pause could also be that the speaker is deciding whether to use a euphemism or not. The point is that we don't really _know_ what particulars underlie a use of _well_, though some such particulars

- 164 -

are often suggested by, or overtly present in, the context.

[4]Svartvik (1980) offers some interesting exploratory comments on intonation patterns associated with _well_.

Chapter 5

[1]This item has several phonological variants, including (yunð), (y nð), and (yð). The question of which variants occur in what discourse, phonological, and syntactic environments is not considered here. There is at least no straightforward correlation between any of these variants and the distinction drawn in this chapter between YKa and YKb. Both types occur in full and reduced forms.

[2]As 'verbal garbage', YK is often classed with _like_ (Chapter 3). This grouping finds its way into the popular literature on speech abuse in Newman's claim that YK and _like_ are "much the same thing" (1974:15). As a comparison of the conclusions of Chapters 3 and 5 will indicate, YK and _like_ are in fact quite different in function and distribution.

[3]Not discussed here is a monograph on YK by Östman (1981), which was received after this dissertation was written. Östman's book is briefly reviewed in Schourup 1984.

[4]These trees are drawn as Ross drew them, with the verb first. This practice has since been abandoned.

[5]As Knowles points out, the constraint is semantic, not syntactic. Consider: _John, I don't doubt, will win the race_.

[6]Though superficially identical, _y(ou) see_ differs from YK

in that only the former is necessarily cohesive. Thus (a) would be bizarre as the first utterance in a conversation, while (b) would not:

    (a)   Y'see, there's nothing like a Coke.
    (b)   Y'know, there's nothing like a Coke.

[7] YK is acceptable in these cases if, for example, Hello is understood as a quotation. YK is frequently used in the present data for unquoting.

[8] The usual restrictions on where speakers may insert inter-jectional pauses, however, remain in force (cf. 3.5).

[9] Claims that intial YK is an attention-getting device used in pretopical position square nicely with the core use of YKb. The presumption of shared ground prior to issuing any contentive material has the effect of asserting something about the addressee's state of mind--namely its predicta-bility in one respect. Speakers approach the matter of as-serting the mental contents of others who are present gin-gerly. The potential face-threat involved with YK is nor-mally attenuated by the obviously sociable intent of the speaker, but if intimacy is undesired by the addressee, the potential for offense is still present.

[10] This passage is an expansion of the propositional consti-tuents of a segment of natural conversation, but it serves here to illustrate the point being made.

[11] The fact that there are cases where a turn change occurs just after YK would not, itself, constitute even weak evi-dence for the claim that YK is a turn signal. Statistical evidence is required, since turn change can occur at any point. What must be shown is that turn change is more likely after a tag-positioned YK than at other points.

[12]This view of _uh_ is consistent with what is known about its positions of occurrence in conversation. No reliable differences have been found between the positions of occurrence of filled and unfilled pauses. It is known that unfilled pauses tend to occur at constituent boundaries, before the first content words of a phonological phrase, and bisecting major constituents (see Boomer 1965, Rochester 1973, and, especially, Grosjean et al. 1979).

[13]Only the two most frequently occurring conjunctions in the present data were counted: _and_ and _but_. No other conjunctions approach these in text frequency.

Chapter 6

[1]It is interesting, though probably not very fruitful, to ask how the addressee is to _know_ whether his or her understanding matches the intent of the speaker.

[2]Of course, much is left unsaid in conversation in general, but this is not _indicated_ by most of the items we use in talk.

[3]As the reader will have already gathered, the conversational 'now' is not a single point in time; it has dimension and can contain, at least, a whole utterance.

[4]_Now_ can be embedded in an utterance it 'introduces':

> There were, now, three bears in that part of the forest.

[5]Because it is tied to the present speaker's moment of utterance and because it is used predominantly as an initi-

ator, <u>now</u> enquotes (see Ch. 2):

> She thought there were typewriters in Greece at that time.
> She thought now there were typewriters in Greece at that time.

[6]Other kinds of lexical items also require contextual interpretation (for example, deictic terms) but are not tied to the present moment of utterance and cannot be viewed as intrusions from the private world.

[7]<u>I mean</u> also occasionaly follows the clarification it announces:

> There were five <u>apples</u> in the basket, I mean.

[8]The term 'addressee', used throughout this study, is not entirely acceptable, but then neither are 'listener', 'interlocutor', 'auditor', 'hearer', etc. What is needed is a term to refer to 'some attentive (even if not actively contributing) participant in a conversation, other than the current speaker.'

REFERENCES

Atlas, J. 1977. Negation, ambiguity, and presupposition. Linguistics and Philosophy 1.321-36.

Banfield, Ann. 1973. Narrative style and the grammar of direct and indirect speech. Foundations of Language 10.1.1-40.

Bernstein, Basil. 1961a. Social class and linguistic development: a theory of social learning. In Education, economy and society, A. H. Halsey, J. Fluid, and A. Anderson (eds.).

----- 1961b. Social structure, language and learning. Educational Research 3.

----- 1962a. Social class, linguistic codes, and grammatical elements. Language and Speech 5.221-40.

----- 1962b. Linguistic codes, hesitation phenomena and intelligence. Language and Speech 5.31-46.

Boomer, Donald S. 1965. Hesitation phenomena and grammatical encoding. Language and Speech 8.148-9.

Butters, Ronald R. 1980. Go 'say'. American Speech 55.304-7.

Bryant, Margaret M. (ed.). 1962. Current American usage. Funk and Wagnalls: New York.

Chafe, Wallace L. (ed.). 1980. The pear stories: cognitive, cultural and linguistic aspects of narrative production. Ablex: Norwood, New Jersey.

Clark, Herbert H. and Wade French. 1981. Telephone 'goodbyes'. Language in Society 10.1-19.

Copperud, Roy H. 1980. American usage and style. Van Nostrand Reinhold: New York.

Coulmas, Florian (ed.) 1981. Conversational routine. Mouton: The Hague.

Crystal, David and Derek Davy. 1975. Advanced conversational English. Longman: London.

DuBois, J. W. 1974. Syntax in mid-sentence. Berkeley studies in syntax and semantics V.1:III(1-25). Institute of Human Learning, Department of Linguistics, University of California, Berkeley.

Duncan, Starkey, Jr. and Donald W. Fiske. 1977. Face-to-face interaction. Lawrence Erlbaum Associates: Hillsdale, New Jersey.

Follett, Wilson. 1966. Modern American usage: a guide. Hill and Wang: New York.

Freeland, L. S. 1951. Language of the Sierra Miwok. Suppl. to International Journal of American Linguistics 17.1. Indiana University Publications in Anthropology and Linguistics. Memoir #6 of I.J.A.L.

----- and Sylvia M. Broadbent. 1960. Central Sierra

Miwok dictionary with texts. University of California Publications in Linguistics V.23. University of California Press: Berkeley.

Fries, Charles C. 1952. The structure of English. Harcourt Brace and World: New York/Burlingame.

Garfinkel, Harold. 1964 (1972). Studies of the routine grounds of everyday activities. Social Problems 11.3 (Reprinted in Sudnow).

Goffman, Erving. 1976. Replies and responses. Language in Society 5.257-313.

----- 1978. Response cries. Language 54.4.787-815.

Goldberg, Julia A. 1976. The syntax, semantics, pragmatics and sociolinguistics of some conventionalized parenthetical clauses in English: 'you know' and 'I mean'. Unpublished diploma dissertation, Department of Linguistics, Cambridge University (England).

----- 1980. Discourse particles: an analysis of the role of 'you know', 'I mean', 'well', and 'actually' in conversation. Ph.D. dissertation, Cambridge University (England).

----- 1981a. Track that topic with 'y'know'! Paper presented to the 1981 Summer Conference on Conversational Interaction and Discourse Processes. University of Nebraska, Lincoln.

-----1981b. Hey, y'know, have I got a topic for you. Unpublished paper.

Goodwin, C. 1975. The interactive construction of the sentence within the turn at talk in natural conversation. In Everyday language: studies in ethnomethodology, G. Psathas (ed.). Irvington: New York.

Grice, H. P. 1967 (1975). William James Lectures. Published in part as 'Logic and conversation' in Syntax and semantics 3 (speech acts), P. Cole and J. L. Morgan (eds.), 1975, 41-58. Seminar Press: New York.

Grosjean, Francois, Lysiane Grosjean, and Harlan Lane. 1979. The patterns of silence: performance structures in sentence production. Cognitive Psychology 11.58-81.

Hines, Carole P. 1977. "Well,...". The Fourth Lacus Forum, Michel Paradis (ed.), 303-318. Hornbeam Press: Columbia, South Carolina.

House, Juliane and Gabriele Kasper. 1981. Politeness markers in English and German. In Coulmas.

Jackendoff, Ray. 1972. Semantic interpretation in generative grammar. M.I.T. Press: Cambridge, Massachusetts.

James, Deborah. 1972. Some aspects of the syntax and semantics of interjections. Papers from the Eighth Regional Meeting of the Chicago Linguistic Society, P.

Peranteau et al. (eds.).

----- 1973. Another look at, say, some grammatical constraints on, oh, interjections and hesitations.
Papers from the Ninth Regional Meeting of the Chicago Linguistic Society, C. Corum et al. (eds.).

----- 1974. The syntax and semantics of some English interjections. University of Michigan dissertation.
University of Michigan Papers in Linguistics 1.3.

----- 1978. The use of 'oh', 'ah', 'say', and 'well' in
relation to a number of grammatical phenomena. Papers
in Linguistics 11/3-4.517-35.

Jefferson, Gail. 1972. Side sequences. In Sudnow.

----- 1973. A case of precision timing in ordinary conversation. Semiotica 9.1.47-96.

----- 1974. Error correction as an interactional resource.
Language in Society 3.2.181-99.

----- 1978. Sequential aspects of storytelling in conversation. In Schenkein.

Jespersen, Otto. 1923. Language: its nature, development
and origin. Allen and Unwin: London.

Joseph, Brian D. 1981. Hittite iwar, wa(r), and Sanskrit
iva. Zeitschrift für vergleichende Sprachforschung
95.93-98.

----- and Lawrence Schourup. 1982. More on (i)wa(r).
Zeitschrift für vergleichende Sprachforschung 96.
56-58.

Keller, Eric. 1981. Gambits: conversational strategy
signals, In Coulmas.

Kempson, R. M. 1980. Ambiguity and word meaning. In
Studies in English linguistics, S. Greenbaum, G. Leech
and J. Svartvik (eds.), 7-16. Longman: London.

----- and Annabel Cormack. 1981. Ambiguity and quantification. Linguistics and Philosophy 4.2.259-310.

Knowles, John. 1980. The tag as a parenthetical. Studies
in Language 4.3.379-409.

Krapp, George P. 1925. The English language in America.

Labov, William and David Fanshel. 1977. Therapeutic discourse: psychotherapy as conversation. Free Press:
New York.

Lakoff, George. 1972. Hedges: a study in meaning criteria
and the logic of fuzzy concepts. Papers from the
Eighth Regional Meeting of the Chicago Linguistic Society, P. Peranteau et al. (eds.).

Lakoff, Robin T. 1973. Questionable answers and answer-
able questions. In Papers in Honour of Henry and
Renée Kahane, B. Kachru (ed.). University of Illinois
Press: Urbana. 453-467.

----- 1974. Linguistic theory and the real world. Berkeley Studies in Syntax and Semantics, V. 1, Department
of Linguistics and Institute of Human Learning, Uni-

versity of California, Berkeley.

Landy, Eugene E. 1971. The underground dictionary. Simon and Schuster: New York.

Lanyon-Orgill, Peter A. 1960. A grammar of the Raluana language. Published by the author: 1701 Beach Drive, Victoria B.C., Canada.

Laver, John. 1981. Linguistic routines and politeness in greeting and parting. In Coulmas.

Literary Digest. 1937. 1.1/1.24 (December 11). No. 22.8-9. Like disliked: of the President's abuse of 'like' and of other presidents' difficulties with formal diction.

Lomas, Charles W. and Ralph Richardson. 1956. Speech: idea and delivery. Houghton Mifflin: Boston.

MacDonnell, A. 1971. A Vedic grammar for students. Oxford University Press: Bombay.

Major, Clarence. 1970. Dictionary of Afro-American slang. International Publishers: New York.

Malinowski, B. 1946. The problem of meaning in primitive languages. Supplement I to Meaning of meaning, C. K. Ogden and I. A. Richards (eds.). Routeledge and Keegan Paul: London.

Matisoff, James A. 1973. The grammar of Lahu. University of California Publications in Linguistics 75. University of California Press: Berkeley.

Murray, Dinah. 1979. Well. Linguistic Inquiry 10.727-732.

Newman, Edwin. 1974. A civil tongue. Bobbs-Merrill: Indianapolis.

----- 1975. Strictly speaking: will America be the death of English? Warner Books.

Östman, Jan-Ola. 1981. 'You know': a discourse functional study. John Benjamins: Amsterdam.

Oxford English Dictionary. 1933. Clarendon Press: Oxford, England.

Partridge, Eric. 1970. A dictionary of slang and unconventional usage. Macmillan: New York.

Rochester, S. R. 1973. The significance of pauses in spontaneous speech. Journal of Psycholinguistic Research 2.51-81.

Ross, John R. 1973. Slifting. In The formal analysis of natural languages, M. Gross, M. Halle and M. P. Schutzenberger (eds.). Mouton: The Hague.

Rotenberg, Joel. 1978. The syntax of phonology. Ph.D. dissertation, M.I.T., Linguistics.

Sachs, J. S. 1967. Recognition memory for syntactic and semantic aspects of connected discourse. Perception and Psychophysics 2.437-42.

Sacks, Harvey; Emanuel A. Schegloff; and Gail Jefferson.

1974. A simplest systematics for the organization of turn taking for conversation. Language 50.4.696-735.

Sadock, Jerrold M. 1969. Hypersentences. Papers in Linguistics 1.2.283-370.

Schegloff, Emanuel A. 1968. Sequencing in conversational openings. American Anthropologist 70.1075-95.

----- 1978. The relevance of repair to syntax-for-conversation. Ms., Department of Sociology, University of California at Los Angeles (cit. by Goldberg 1980).

----- 1981. Discourse and conversation: 'uh huh' and other things that come between sentences. Paper read at Georgetown University Round Table on Languages and Linguistics, 3/20/81.

----- and Harvey Sacks. 1973. Opening up closings. Semiotica 8.289-327.

-----; Gail Jefferson; and Harvey Sacks. 1977. The preference for self-correction in the organization of repair in conversation. Language 53.2.361-382.

Schenkein, Jim (ed.). 1978. Studies in the organization of conversational interaction. Academic Press: New York.

Schiffrin, Deborah. 1981a. Tense variation in narrative. Language 57.45-62.

----- 1981b. Accountability in discourse analysis: the case of 'now'. Paper read at New Ways of Analyzing Variation in English X, 10/24/81, Philadelphia, Pennsylvania.

Schourup, Lawrence. 1982. Quoting with go 'say'. American Speech 57.2.148-9.

----- 1984. Book notice: Östman, Jan-Ola. 1981. 'You know': a discourse-functional approacn. Language 60.3.665-6.

Sharrock, W. W. and R. Turner. 1978. On a conversational environment for equivocality. In Schenkein.

Shimanoff, S. and J. Brunak. 1977. Repair in planned and unplanned discourse. Discourse across time and space, O. Keenan and T. L. Bennett (eds.). Southern California Occasional Papers in Linguistics #5, May 1977. Department of Linguistics, University of Southern California, Los Angeles.

Stubbs, Michael. 1983. Discourse analysis: the sociolinguistic analysis of natural language. Basil Blackwell: Oxford.

Sudnow, David (ed.) 1972. Studies in social interaction. Free Press: New York.

Svartvik, Jan. 1980. 'Well' in conversation. Studies in English for Randolph Quirk, Sidney Greenbaum et al. (eds.). Longman: London.

Tannen, Deborah. 1979. Toward a theory of conversational

style: the machine-gun question. Paper read at the Annual Meeting of the Linguistic Society of America, 12/27/79, Los Angeles, California.

----- and Piyale Comert Öztek. 1981. Health to our mouths: formulaic expressions in Turkish and Greek. In Coulmas.

Urdang, Laurence. 1979. Replies. American Speech 54.77-79.

Urmson, J. D. 1963. Parenthetical verbs. Philosophy and ordinary language, C. E. Caton (ed.). University of Illinois Press: Urbana.

Wanner, E. 1974. On remembering, forgetting, and understanding sentences. Mouton: The Hague.

Webster's New Collegiate Dictionary. 1979. G. and C. Merriam Co.: Springfield, Massachusetts.

Webster's Third New International Dictionary. 1966. G. and C. Merriam Co.: Springfield, Massachusetts.

Wentworth, Harold and Stuart Berg Flexner. 1960. A dictionary of American slang. Thomas Y. Crowell: New York.

White, William. 1955. Wayne State University Slang. American Speech 30.4.301-5.

Whitman, C. Dale. 1974. 'Like' as a conjunction. American Speech 49. 1/2.156-8.

Wood, Frederick T. and Robert J. Hill. 1979. Dictionary of English colloquial idioms. A. Wheaton: Exeter, England.

Woolford, E. 1979. The developing complementizer system of Tok Pisin: syntactic change in progress. In The genesis of language, K. Hill (ed.). (The First Michigan Colloquium). Karoma: Ann Arbor.

Wright, Thomas. 1857. Dictionary of obsolete and provincial English. Henry G. Bohn: London. (Reprinted 1967: Gale Research Co., Detroit).

Zwicky, Arnold M. and Jerrold Sadock. 1973. Ambiguity tests and how to fail them. Ohio State University Working Papers in Linguistics 16.1-36.